GODFREY WALTON

CREDIT ✖ SECRETS

THE STEP-BY-STEP EASY AND COMPLETE GUIDE
to Rebuild Your Credit Score and Improve Your Personal
Finance with The Best Strategies and Techniques
to Raise Your Credit Line

COPYRIGHT - 2021 -

ALL RIGHTS RESERVED.

The content contained within this book may not be reproduced, duplicated or transmitted without direct written permission from the author or the publisher. Under no circumstances will any blame or legal responsibility be held against the publisher, or author, for any damages, reparation, or monetary loss due to the information contained within this book. Either directly or indirectly.

LEGAL NOTICE:

This book is copyright protected. This book is only for personal use. You cannot amend, distribute, sell, use, quote or paraphrase any part, or the content within this book, without the consent of the author or publisher.

DISCLAIMER NOTICE:

Please note the information contained within this document is for educational and entertainment purposes only. All effort has been executed to present accurate, up to date, and reliable, complete information. No warranties of any kind are declared or implied. Readers acknowledge that the author is not engaging in the rendering of legal, financial, medical or professional advice. The content within this book has been derived from various sources. Please consult a licensed professional before attempting any techniques outlined in this book.

By reading this document, the reader agrees that under no circumstances is the author responsible for any losses, direct or indirect, which are incurred as a result of the use of information contained within this document, including, but not limited to, - errors, omissions, or inaccuracies.

TABLE OF CONTENTS

INTRODUCTION	5
CHAPTER 1 What Is A Credit Score?	9
CHAPTER 2 How to Assess Your Financial Situation?	21
CHAPTER 3 Reducing Current Expenses and Debts	33
CHAPTER 4 Ways to Raise Money to Pay Debts	45
CHAPTER 5 Ways to Improve Your Credit History	63
CHAPTER 6 Choosing Credit Cards	77
CHAPTER 7 How to Protect Yourself?	85
CONCLUSION	95

Introduction

It's quick to go into debt during a downturn in the economy, and it's much harder to get out of it. Missed payments, defaults, repossessions, and even foreclosures and bankruptcy are all consequences of mounting loans, and they finally show up on the credit report.

Poor credit may have a wide range of consequences in your life. You can encounter difficulties:

- Obtaining a financial loan
- Obtaining a market-new credit card
- Getting a bank account
- If you're renting a house
- Receiving an employment offer

If you have open-ended financial accounts, such as credit cards, and the credit scores decline, the insurer is likely to raise the interest rate, lower your credit cap, or terminate your credit rights. And if you're looking for fresh loans, you'll almost certainly spend a lot more in interest and penalties than those who have decent credit. Having poor credit may also result in higher auto insurance premiums.

This will create a vicious spiral in which your poor credit keeps you from doing the same stuff that would help you get back on your feet financially. However, by taking steps to improve your credit, you will interrupt the loop.

If you've missed payments, been prosecuted, threatened repossession or eviction, or even claimed bankruptcy, this book will show you how to restore your credit in a clear and efficient manner. You'll learn how to create a schedule, bargain with banks, tidy up the credit record, and go ahead with positive credit. Bear these vital facts in mind when you read this material and determine how to manage the situation.

You are not the only one that feels this way. Many individuals are affected by financial difficulties. Unemployment is also a concern, and disposable incomes and investments are yet to rebound from the recession. Millions of decent, hardworking individuals are having difficulty covering their bills, the same people who earn credit deals on a regular basis.

You are protected by the law. Knowing and asserting your privileges will help you get rid of bill collectors and start again financially. Debtors who fight back are more likely to have additional time to compensate, get late payments waived, get loans settled for less than the entire sum owed, and get derogatory points stripped on their credit records.

It's something you should manage on your own. The book's material and forms are valid in all 50 states as well as the District of Columbia. You don't have to pay for credit restoration facilities if you obey the instructions; in fact, you'll be better off if you don't. In certain cases, you would not need the services of a lawyer. However, you might need or wish to speak with a lawyer under some circumstances. When do you contact a lawyer? This book can tell you when it's a smart time to do so.

Nobody's credit is severely compromised. If you have had a loop of bad luck financially, you can believe you'll never be able to get credit again. That obviously isn't the case. As long as your financial difficulties are behind you, you should be able to obtain small forms of credit very easily. You should be able to restore the reputation sufficiently to get a big credit card or loan within one to two years. Many banks are able to lend credibility to individuals who have improved their financial status, even though their credit history isn't perfect.

This book goes into credit restoration in great detail. Easy-to-use forms assist you with calculating your obligations, planning a schedule, bargaining with creditors or bill collectors, and communicating with credit rating services, both of which may be intimidating jobs. (At the last of the book, there is a table with instructions about how to retrieve forms from a website.) You'll be able to restore your credit and pave the way for a brighter financial future if you use this material.

Chapter 1
What Is A Credit Score?

Today, most creditors use credit ratings to assess your credit history, which is stored in your credit files and recorded in your credit reports (as discussed above, your credit scores are based on information in your credit reports). We'll look at how banks and credit rating agencies score the details in your report to determine your credit score and also why paying for your credit score may not be worth it.

WHAT IS A CREDIT SCORE?

Credit scores are numerical estimates that are meant to reflect the probability of you losing a payment. An organization collects details on your financial background, such as how many transactions you have, if you pay on schedule, collection activities against you, and so on, then measures you to those with identical profiles and assigns you points depending on your creditworthiness. A high credit score means that you are low risk, that is, you are more able to repay a loan, while a low credit score suggests that you will have issues. In certain cases, your wage, profession, title, workplace, date of employment, or job experience are not taken into observation while calculating your credit score.

WHO USES CREDIT SCORES?

Many companies look at credit scores in approving credit and also in determining credit terms and interest rates.

Lenders use your credit scores to check whether to extend your new credit, either to increase or decrease an existing line of credit, once it will be easy to collect from you on an outstanding account and even whether you are likely to file for bankruptcy. The vast majority of mortgage lenders rely on credit scores, as do car dealers, credit card issuers, and insurance companies. And increasingly, utility companies and even cell phone companies use credit scores to determine whether and how much of a deposit to require. Your credit score determines not only whether you'll get the loan but also what your interest rate and credit terms will be: The lower your score, the higher your interest rate is likely to be.

HOW ARE CREDIT SCORES CALCULATED?

Creditors can choose to buy credit scores from a variety of companies that sell different types of credit scores. Most credit scores range from 300 to 400 up to 800 to 990, depending on the type of score. Some models have been in use for years; others are new. Some credit scores are designed for use on particular kinds of credit, e.g., auto loans, mortgages, or credit cards.

Your credit score may be different based on the company that generates it, the information considered, and the reason for the creation of the score. But the key ideas behind scoring are very simple. Here are some of the major credit scoring companies and the factors they consider in developing scores.

FICO SCORES

The largest and most ubiquitous credit scoring company is the Fair Isaac Corporation, which goes by the name of FICO. It is the company that generates FICO scores. FICO claims (and industry analysts agree) that over 90% of credit decisions are made using its scores. Because Freddie Mac, Fannie Mae, and the FHA require some version of a FICO score for mortgages they purchase or insure, today, most mortgage lenders rely on FICO scores rather than other companies' credit scores. A different name is used for FICO scores prepared for each of the three credit reporting agencies. At Equifax, it's called the BEACON Score; at Experian, the Experian/FICO Risk Model; and at TransUnion, the Risk Score of FICO (formerly known as EMPIRICA).

The factors FICO considers in coming up with credit scores include:

- Payment history (about 35% of the score). The company looks at such things as whether you have paid on time, have any delinquent accounts, have declared bankruptcy, had a foreclosure, and how recent past due accounts are and whether you have judgments against you. This is the largest part of your score, so it is the most important. According to FICO, collection account, late payments, repossessions, settled accounts, public record items, and foreclosures, like judgments, tax liens, or bankruptcies, can create a negative value to your FICO score. And even making a payment only one month late can negatively affect your score.

- Amounts owed on credit accounts (about 30% of the score). FICO looks at such things as the amounts you owe and how many of your accounts carry a balance. Your score will be low if you owe something to your credit limits. Paying down your outstanding debt is the main way to improve this part of your score. Even if you pay off your credit card each month, your credit score will likely be based on the amount you owed on your last credit statement.

- The length of your credit history (about 15% of the score). Generally, a longer credit history yields a higher score.

- New credit (about 10% of the score). FICO likes to see an established credit history rather than a lot of new accounts. Opening different types of accounts in a short period of time might indicate a higher risk. Depending on the factors, hard inquiries on your accounts can even lower your ratings. If some creditors search your credit report, for example, it can seem as if you are desperately trying to find fresh credit. This is why it's crucial to exercise caution when applying for new credit. And if you're just window browsing, used car sellers can attempt to get you to sign a document for them to check your credit score. If you're adamant about making a bargain, don't commit to this. But as long as you do all of your comparison shopping for a car, home mortgage, or student loan within about 30 days or so, it shouldn't have much effect on your score. (Older versions of FICO use 14 days; the newest version uses 45 days. But you won't know which version any particular lender is using.) Don't get overly concerned about inquiries. Inquiries make up only a small part of your FICO score. According to FICO, the number of inquiries is not usually a major factor in your credit score; an inquiry would likely lower your score by fewer than 5 points, even if outside of a short comparison-shopping period. And FICO says it does not include an inquiry in its score once it is older than 12 months.

- Credit types (about 10% of the score). FICO is looking for a "healthy mix" of different types of credit, both revolving accounts (such as credit cards) and installment accounts (like a mortgage or car loan).

Sometimes people worry unnecessarily that other kinds of information may affect their scores. But, as an example, none of the following are included in FICO scores: your age, salary, occupation, title, employer, date employed, employment history, child or family support obligations, rental agreements, or whether you are participating in credit counseling.

You can see that about 65% of your FICO score depends on whether you pay your bills on time (35%) and whether the amount you owe is too high in relation to your credit limits (30%). Because FICO also offers a variety of FICO scoring formulas that emphasize different aspects of your credit, you may have more than one FICO score. And because a FICO score is based on what is in your credit report and each of the three nationwide credit reporting agencies may have somewhat different information about you, each credit reporting company may have a different credit score for you.

WHAT'S A GOOD FICO SCORE?

FICO scores range from 300 to 850. In early 2016, FICO reported that the average score was just under 700. Most lenders would consider 700 to be pretty good. A high FICO score is generally above 750. Scores over 800 are considered excellent.

According to Equifax, the portion of the general population that falls within various credit score ranges is as follows (although Equifax no longer calls these "FICO score ranges," these numbers are the same as those it previously listed as FICO score ranges):

- 20% are above 780
- 20% are in the range of 745-780
- 20% are in the range of 690-745
- 20% are in the range of 620-690
- 20% are below 619

FICO offers a free calculator you can use to see how different credit scores may affect how much it costs you to get credit.

CREDIT FILE FITNESS: A NEW TYPE OF MORTGAGE SCORING

More and more adults, millennials, for example, are remaining at home with their parents before purchasing their first house. Although this approach allows young adults with stable jobs to save money, what's often lacking is strong credit history. One reason for this is a preference for debit cards over credit cards. The downfall is that exclusive debit card use doesn't allow someone to demonstrate a pattern of appropriate credit usage. Therefore, a potential borrower without an established credit history will often find it difficult to get a mortgage.

To account for this, some lenders now look to "credit file fitness." This approach takes into account a person's credit score along with a steady employment record and a history of paying off other debt, such as a car loan or student loans. For this reason, anyone without an extensive credit history who would like to buy a house should pay such debts in a timely manner.

MOST COMMON REASONS FOR NEGATIVE CREDIT DECISIONS

According to Equifax, below are the most common factors that negatively affect credit decisions, and you can see how these fit with the way credit files are scored:

- Serious delinquency

- Serious delinquency and public record filed or collection initiated

- Time since delinquency too recent or unknown

- Level of delinquency on accounts too high

- Number of accounts with delinquency too high

- The amount owed on accounts too high

- Percentage of balances to credit limits on revolving accounts too high

- Length of time accounts has been established too short
- Too many accounts with balances

HOW MUCH CREDIT SCORE DO YOU NEED TO GET A CREDIT?

What credit score a creditor requires in order to extend credit or to provide the best interest rates and credit terms is usually not made public. However, you can use FICO's calculator to estimate how different FICO scores might affect credit offers you receive. Often, information about this topic is based on best guesses. But here is how some agencies and companies extend credit (or insure loans) based on credit scores. This provides a good indication of how credit scores relate to available credit.

FANNIE MAE

Fannie Mae is a large government-controlled company that buys a large percentage of mortgages in the country. If lenders want to be able to sell their loans to Fannie Mae, they must meet Fannie Mae's guidelines.

Fannie Mae requires lenders to use the "classic FICO" credit score, if possible, to measure credit. The classic FICO score is also called these names at the different credit reporting agencies:

- Equifax Beacon® 5.0
- Experian/Fair Isaac Risk Model V2SM
- TransUnion FICO® Risk Score, Classic 04

As of 2016, Fannie Mae generally required a credit score of 620 for fixed-rate loans to be insured by the federal government and 640 for adjustable-rate mortgages. Of course, lenders may also have their own requirements that are more stringent than Fannie Mae's.

THE FEDERAL HOUSING ADMINISTRATION

The Federal Government (FHA), which is part of the United States Department of Health and Human Development, insures mortgages in order to allow developers to make home-buying loans. It has different criteria depending on the amount of down payment. Borrowers with FICO scores below 580 must make at least a 10% down payment.

Those with scores of 580 or higher need only a 3.5% down payment. Applicants with credit scores below 500 are not eligible for FHA insurance. Lenders themselves may have more stringent requirements, and people with low scores are likely to be charged higher interest.

EXPERIAN AUTOMOTIVE

Experian Automotive's report for the fourth quarter of 2016 analyzing auto loans showed how many loans are made to borrowers with lower credit ratings. About 20% of car loans went to those whose credit scores were above 781. About 40% of car loans went to those with scores of 661 to 780. About 20% of loans went to borrowers with scores of 601 to 660; about 17% of loans went to borrowers with scores of 501 to 600, and about 3% of the loans went to borrowers with scores below 500. Experian found the average credit score for a new car customer was 711, and for a used car buyer was 654.

GETTING YOUR CREDIT SCORE

In some situations, a creditor must provide you with the credit score it relied on a credit transaction or decision. You can also pay to get your credit score. But as we explain below, it is probably not worth the money to do so.

WHEN CAN YOU GET YOUR CREDIT SCORE FOR FREE?

In certain cases, a credit score is required in order to complete a credit transaction. When you are entitled to a free credit score, the agency that provides it would normally often inform you of the following:

- The number of available scores under the scoring model that was used to produce your score.

- The score's creation date.

- Company's name or organization that produced the score (for example, FICO). Here are some scenarios in which you should get a free credit score.

You submit a form for a home loan. When you qualify for a loan on residential property and the lender uses a credit score, the lender must report your credit score and any of the variables that adversely influenced your score, in order of priority (up to four; five if one of the factors is the number of inquiries). The lender must also supply you with instructions about how to reach the credit rating service that issued the ratings. Fannie Mae typically allows lenders who wish to market their loans to Fannie Mae to obtain a FICO credit score from one of the three national credit monitoring services, which suggests you'd have to learn all three ratings.

Lenders that use automatic programs to review loan applications that contain details other than what is in a credit file or who obtain a credit score from a firm other than a credit reporting agency may have a credit score from a credit-reporting agency instead of the score they actually used.

A credit report recipient takes a negative move against you. If a recipient of your credit report depended on a credit score before taking adverse action against you as of August 15, 2011, the credit score must be revealed. When a borrower does the following actions:

- Refuses to give you a credit limit increase.

- Declines to offer you credit in the amount you demanded.

- Closes the account.

- Changes the conditions of your account in an unfavorable way (but does not change the terms of all, or substantially all, other consumer accounts of the same type).

Creditors, as well as those that have a right to access your credit report and ratings, such as banks, government departments who offer permits or benefits, employees, tenants, and other customers, must reveal your credit score whether they use it to take unfavorable action against you in some way. If you initiate a contract and the recipient makes adverse adjustments to your health, government services, housing, rental terms, or any account, you are subject to this provision.

Your credit report and score recipient would also inform you of the main variables that negatively impacted your credit score (up to four; five if one of the factors is the number of inquiries). If the adverse conduct is relevant to credit, the borrower may either provide you with the precise grounds for its judgment or notify you that you have the right to apply for them.

You are charged a higher interest rate from a trustee. If a borrower owes you a higher average percentage rate (APR) than it charges anyone, it must send you a note (called a "risk-based pricing" notice) informing you of the real credit score is used to make the credit judgment as of August 15, 2011. If the borrower used several credit scores, you just need to know about one of them. The borrower must therefore inform you of the major factors that have harmed your credit score (up to four; five if they include the number of inquiries as a factor). Under certain situations, this provision applies whether a creditor uses a credit report and a credit score to determine what standard APR to charge on fresh or current credit and gives you a cost that is lower than the rate it offers about 40% of other customers who have received comparable credit.

If the creditor instead discloses to any individual who demands credit the person's existing credit score or the most recent credit score determined by a credit rating service for the purpose of expanding credit, the creditor can postpone sending you the note of the original credit score it relies on.

Other restrictions and constraints apply to the risk-based price warning provision. Under certain situations, the borrower is not required to inform you about the credit score is used or a new credit score. The following are the main limitations and exceptions:

If the creditor granted you credit on the terms you requested, the creditor is not required to follow the notice rules.

- A creditor who sends you an "adverse action" notice is not obligated to follow through.

- The mortgage you applied for is backed by one to four units of residential real estate, and the borrower sends you a note that includes your credit score as well as other details.

- A borrower only has to assess APR prices on a given form of credit to make a decision (such as student loans, new car loans, or variable rate home loans).

- A creditor who gives you a credit card deal that is only provided to buyers with poor credit ratings, for example, is not required to warn you of any credit card deals it provides.

- A borrower must only compare standard APRs and not any other prices. As a result, it might allow credit card deals to a community of people of the same daily APR, but give each of them a package with a different interest rate than the one it applies to other late-paying customers, and it doesn't have to say you.

If a creditor uses a credit score and gives you an APR that is less attractive than what it offers to around 40% of other customers, the creditor is required to report your credit score unless all of the exceptions or restrictions mentioned above apply.

Chapter 2
How to Assess Your Financial Situation?

You can believe you have a decent estimate of how much money you make and how much money you owe. You may even be scared of seeing how poor your financial condition is. The reality is that you'll need more than a rough idea of your financial situation to move through the nitty-gritty of credit repair. Instead, you can calculate your monthly salary, monthly interest contributions, the balance of your unpaid debt, any sums you owe (if any), and any monthly expenditures. Here's how to do it.

TOTAL UP YOUR INCOME

Gather the paystubs and all other income-related records, as well as a calculator.

Require income reports for all of you whether you are married or living with someone with whom you share expenses. If you are paying more often than once a month, use Form F-9 to translate your salary to a monthly number. If you don't get the same number per month, take the average of the previous 12 months. The average is then entered. Leave it blank if you do not have any sources of income mentioned. This is an income-only type. So, if you get child care, add it; but, if you pay child support, leave it blank. It will be entered into a different type. If you have revenue from sources other than those mentioned on the document, mention it under Other.

When you've finished detailing all of your earnings, sum up your and your spouse's earnings for each line and enter the total in Column 4. Add up the totals in a column. And apply the Net Income for Columns 2 and 3 as a confirmation. The number should be the same as Column 4's total. Column 4 adds up to the gross net monthly revenue.

DETERMINE YOUR DEBT PAYMENTS AND TOTAL DEBT

Now it's time to work out how much money you owe. Use Type F-10, Your Debts, to keep track of your debts (see the table at the end of this book to understand forms). Get a calculator and gather the records that display your bills, the cumulative sum you owe, and any amounts that are past due, including any fines or penalties that have been applied. Include any arrangements you can't break without a charge, such as a phone or a gym deal

that lasts a few months or years, in addition to clear loans like those on your home, vehicle, and credit cards. Include back loans, such as past-due energy costs, particularly though you don't have a daily recurring contribution or a long-term lease for them.

COLUMN 1: DEBTS

In Column 1, write the debt form. And if your loans are withheld from your salary, list them. And if you're not sure which debts you're liable for, include debts for your partner or anyone with whom you share living expenses. It's better to focus on your credit condition as a team while your friendship is still intact.

COLUMN 2: OUTSTANDING BALANCE

Fill in the amount you already owe on each debt in this column. For e.g., if you lent $10,000 and now owe $6,000 on a vehicle, enter $6,000. Join $2,000 if you have a $3,000 doctor's payment that you only owe $2,000 on. You will find out how much you owe for each debt by reviewing the most recent bill:

- Contacting the company's customer support department.
- Accessing your account details through the internet (you may have to register to access your account data).

Many borrowers have electronic telephone networks that instantly supply balance and payment details without asking you to communicate with a live individual. If you really must talk with somebody and are worried about getting harassed by creditors you've been ignoring, just ask for balance details. Explain why you're looking at the choices and ought to see how much you owe before proceeding whether the customer care agent becomes a bill collector. Tell the agent that you can call the organization as quickly as possible but that you just need to see how much you owe right now. Hang up if the delegate continues to bother you. Figure out how much you owe your borrower or wait before the next payment arrives.

There would not be an unpaid balance on any of the obligations you mention, such as child maintenance or homeowner's fees. Simply draw a line across the gap in Column 2 for such.

CREDIT REPAIR SECRETS

COLUMNS 3 AND 4: TOTAL AMOUNT AND MONTHLY PAYMENT YOU ARE BEHIND

Fill in the balance you owe on each debt in Columns 3 and 4. Place the amount you owe in Column 4 and leaving Column 3 blank if you don't have fixed recurring fees, such as for a medical bill. Put the average payment balance in Column 3 whether you make daily monthly payments, such as on a vehicle loan or a mortgage. Place the entire sum you owe in Column 4 if you are late on those payments. Include the number of late fees multiplied by the number of missing payments, as well as any extra costs or fines. If you have no idea know how much you owe, you will possibly find out by going online or calling the creditor's customer support line, the same way you figure out how much you owe. If you can't get an exact number, make the best guess you can.

Enter the monthly minimum necessary charge in Column 3 and the full balance in Column 4 for credit cards. This isn't to say that making just the minimum payment is a healthy long-term strategy. And sure, you don't enter an annual interest payment more than once. If you paid child care by payroll deductions, for example, you already removed it from your salary when you completed Form F-9, so don't include it in Column 3. Include the number in Column 4 if you owe back taxes that aren't getting withheld from your paycheck.

COLUMN 5: IS THE DEBT SECURED?

To assess a debt's priority for settlement and your negotiation plan with the borrower, you'll need to decide if it's protected or unsecured.

Since you risk losing anything of worth if you don't pay a guaranteed mortgage, it's normally the first obligation to pay it off. In Column 5, write down the property that protects each of your covered debts. If you're not positive, check the credit agreement and see if a security interest is included and what the defense is listed as.

COLUMN 6: PRIORITY OF DEBTS

These are the loans that you would settle, and you will face serious repercussions if you do not. Priority loans make up the majority of covered debts. Other loans are a high priority, for instance, and if you don't compensate, the utilities will be cut off, then you will lose your health care.

Even if they are not protected, government-backed student loans could be a medium priority (due to the extreme repercussions of default). The borrower can't seize something from you unless it wins a case and obtains a lien, but certain unsecured loans, such as unsecured credit cards, are actually the lowest concern. In addition, certain unsecured loans may be discharged in bankruptcy if applicable. For the time being, label as "1" the debts you believe are your highest priority, "2" the debts you believe are medium priority, and "3" the debts you believe are low priority. You'll come back to this form in later chapters when you focus on restoring your credit and managing your profits and debts.

COMPARE YOUR INCOME WITH TOTAL DEBTS

Now add the columns in the Your Debts table together. Column 2 indicates the gross amount of debt you owe. Column 3 shows the money you'll need to pay off your minimum credit card debt per month. Column 4 shows the gross amount of back debt you owe.

There are some forms mentioned below which you can download from different websites like www.nolo.com.

Subtract your gross recurring minimum contributions (Column 3) from your total net profits (Column 4 on Form F-9) to get an idea of how much funds you have available per month to fund the remainder of your monthly bills, pay off unpaid loans, and start investing.

TALLY UP MONTHLY LIVING EXPENSES

The next step is to find out how much it would cost. you charge per month to survive, taking into account your daily monthly loan payments from Column 3 of Form F-10 (except for your minimum credit card payments). This figure covers all of the living costs but excludes interest on past-due loans. For instance, you should include your mortgage payment (since this is your monthly housing payment), and if you buy food on a credit card, you should include the whole grocery bill. Begin by filling out Form F-11, Daily Expenses, which allows you to log all of your spendings for a week. Here's how to fill it out:

1. Print nine versions of the questionnaire so you can keep track of your spending over the next 60 days. You can keep track of your finances for a few months and ensure that your expenditure isn't dependent on a few weeks of exceptionally high or low spending. Whether you're married or sharing expenses with others, you can each keep track of your own expenses and sum them up at the end of the week.

2. Start keeping track of your spending on Sunday.

3. Fill in the void at the top of one copy of the form with the date of the Sunday.

4. Have a copy of the week's form with you at all times.

5. Keep track of both cash and credit card purchases. Have checks, ATM withdrawals, gift cards, automated bank withdrawals, and credit card payments. And sure, to factor in bank fees. Deposits into insurance funds, certificates of deposit, or money market accounts, as well as sales of shares such as stocks or bonds, are not included. That's when Type F-12 comes in.

6. Charges incurred on a credit card should be included. Include recurring payments on a credit card for products you've purchased in the past, just not monthly payments on a credit card for products you've changed in the past. Instead, you'll record them on Form F-12. Consider the

following scenario: you have a $1,000 credit card balance, you add $230 in additional payments over four weeks, and you pay $250 on the card in the fourth week. List the $230 based on the dates and services bought ($130 for groceries, $50 for diesel, $35 for cable television, and so on). Power service is $15. However, don't include the $20 you spent for the old balance. The $20 can be used to fill out Form F-12.

7. Put the form away at the end of each week to get a new copy. Return to Step 3. You just need to complete the first four days of the last week.

8. When you've recorded expenditures for 60 days, report any seasonal, monthly, semi-annual, or quarterly expenses you incurred but didn't pay during the two-month tracking cycle in the heading Other Expenses of any sort. Land taxes, vehicle license fees, magazine subscriptions, tax planning fees, and insurance premiums are the most prevalent. Others, though, exist. For e.g., if you keep track of expenditures throughout the winter, don't forget about summer expenses, including your children's camp costs or pool upkeep. Don't neglect to include your annual holiday gift expenditures whether you report in the summer or spring. Consider a wide range of possibilities to be systematic. Examining your check register or credit card statements from the previous year can be beneficial.

Keep track of the money you set aside for savings and debt reduction

To keep a record of how much money you placed into investing or paying off accrued loans, For Payments to Savings and Debt Reduction, use Form F-12. Savings and loans, contributions into savings funds, certificates of deposit, or money market accounts, sales of investments such as securities or bonds, and charges against credit card balances in excess of the normal minimum monthly payments are also examples of this. So, if you have $230 in additional payments on your credit card this month but just pay $250, the additional $20 goes toward that credit card balance, list the $20 on Form F-12. Once a week, use Form F-12 to keep track of your savings and loan payments. You'll need one of the weekly forms for the entire month if you only approve savings and debt reduction payments once a month.

You already withheld sums placed into retirement by payroll deduction, such as funds into a 401k plan, from your wages on Form F-9. Don't subtract it again. Instead, write the form of deduction (such as 401(k)) to help you remember it in your preparation, then leave the Amount blank. For the next 60 days, keep track of the funds you placed into investment and debt reduction.

MAKE A BUDGET

After a couple of months of tracking your costs, revenue, investments, and loan repayment contributions, you're able to make a budget or expenditure schedule. Use the Monthly Budget Form F-13. When it comes to credit repair, the main purpose of creating a budget is to have a better view of your financial condition, which can help you determine the credit repair choices that are best for you. Furthermore, making a budget can assist you in determining where adjustments should be made so that you can meet the daily contributions on schedule and continue eliminating large delinquent balances and past due debts. If you have a record of, repossessions, late payments default, or bankruptcy, the quicker you can establish a track record of on-time payments and reduce your delinquent balances down far within the credit limits, the more your credit will improve. Your most critical method for getting there is your budget.

Your budget would be built on the numbers you entered on Forms F-9, F-11, and F-12.

Take these measures to create and use a monthly budget:

1. Make many copies of the Monthly Budget Form F-13. Making a budget that you can deal with is a trial and error method, and you can need to draft some proposals before you get them correct.

2. Complete Forms F-9, F-11, and F-12, which detail your earnings, spending, and savings/debt reduction.

3. Look over Form F-11's expenditures. They're broken down into categories like housing costs, food, and transportation. You can cross it off, erase it from your computer, or just keep it vacant if you don't have any expenditures in that category. Add a column to a blank line if you have a cost that isn't specified on the form.

4. List the estimated real monthly expenditures in each segment in the first column (labeled Projected). Add up the real expenditures for the two months you tracked, and divide the balance by two to get these figures. (You should only use the recurring payment number for daily monthly expenses, including auto or mortgage payments.) Require a monthly sum for all payments that are seasonal, yearly, or quarterly. For instance, if you pay $3,600 in property taxes each year, this category could have a monthly cost of $300 ($3,600 divided by 12). Don't neglect to include the Form F-12 investment and debt relief payments.

5. Total up all of your estimated monthly spending, investments, and debt reduction, and write it at the bottom of each list. Then sum up all three pages' totals and type them on the line labeled Cumulative Expenses on the last row of Form F-13's Projected column.

6. Enter your estimated monthly revenue (from Form F-9) below your projected net expenditures on the last page of Form F-13.

7. Calculate the difference between your estimated revenue and your projected expenditures. These numbers can assist you in determining your credit recovery choices.

8. Continue to keep track of your monthly spending. In the section next to the Projected column on Form F-13, write the actual month in the heading. Using the expenditure groups, keep track of the expenditures for the month. Go going in the same manner for the next month. Compare

the real expenditures against your estimated expenses per month (or many months a month) to see whether you are sticking under your schedule.

BASED ON YOUR FINANCIAL SITUATION DETERMINING YOUR CREDIT REPAIR OPTIONS

It's time to assess your financial status now that you've determined your wages, living costs, and overall unpaid debt. This book discusses a variety of credit restoration solutions and techniques. Your financial data will assist you in determining which option is better for you.

The majority of citizens would fall into one of the above groups.

YOU FACE A FINANCIAL EMERGENCY

A financial emergency is described as any condition that puts you at risk of being homeless or losing access to essential goods or services. Financial emergencies include a pending relocation, a letter demanding foreclosure, an IRS takeover of your home, a power cut-off, and the possibility of auto repossession. Although receiving a hostile letter or phone call from a bill collector is upsetting, it is not an emergency. Credit restoration isn't a good idea if you're in a hurry. Concentrate on the current emergency scenario. You will return to credit restoration after you've weathered the hurricane (which may take months, a year, or more). Any of the methods for lowering your debts or bargaining with creditors or debt collectors discussed later in the book might be helpful to you. In addition, as part of mediation to address a debt emergency, you will be entitled to minimize the detrimental impact on your credit. However, dealing with the immediate situation is your top priority. Start by calling your creditor and seeing about what you'll need to do to retain your car, house, or other valued property. However, before you commit to something, you can consult with a lawyer to ensure that you are not bringing yourself into further trouble. A new deal for deferred or postponed installments, for example, can make your life simpler right now, but it may also revoke rights you have today, increase the amount of interest you owe dramatically, or grant a borrower additional rights to recover a debt. If a borrower asks you to choose to accept a deposit on an old mortgage or undertake some adjustments to an ongoing loan or deal (other than to limit or postpone payments), an attorney will help you determine if the arrangement can fix or exacerbate the problems.

YOUR LIVING EXPENSES ARE GREATER THAN YOUR INCOME

If your living costs exceed your salary, your first goal should be to get your finances in order. Credit repair is a secondary concern.

In order to stabilize your financial condition, you may need to take steps that may hurt your credit in the short term. You would have to give up your automobile or even your home, for example. It might be necessary to persuade a borrower to record these in a manner that minimizes the harm to your credit, but even if that isn't practicable, keep in mind that the primary objective is to resolve the unpaid debts. Concentrate your efforts on getting a career or another means of money, cutting costs, and paying bills in order to maintain your house, vehicle, and other essentials.

The below are several suggestions for getting out of a financial bind:

- Seeking assistance from a reputable financial specialist.
- Bankruptcy petition
- Speak with a career coach regarding finding work or transitioning to a higher-paying profession.
- Cost reduction
- Use arbitration and settlement to reduce or eliminate debts.

Your credit score can generally increase only when you show creditors that you have gotten back on your feet financially.

You would have the ability to change the location. So, that you can afford your living expenses and other expenditures per month depending on the disparity in your revenue and expenses, the kind of loans you have, if you have enough funds, you may pay or create lump sum settlements, and your persistence in trying to make substantial reductions in your expenses or rises in your salary. If you can slash costs or will current loan commitments when you move through the following chapters, go back to the budget and make the necessary changes. When you're finished, put all new numbers together and get your new net cost number. Your aim is to strike a compromise between your costs and taxes such that your income covers your living expenses.

YOUR EARNINGS ARE ABLE TO COVER YOUR LIVING COSTS

If your monthly salary exceeds your monthly living costs, you've taken a significant move toward improving your credit, getting your personal finances in order. However, the monthly spending is also crucial in determining how much funds you have leftover per month to pay off debts. (And the debt load can be high and daunting for some.) As a result, just as the subsequent chapters assist you in balancing your existing living costs with your revenue, they will also assist you in reducing burdensome unpaid or overdue loans that are needed to restore your credit.

- Freeing up funds to pay off unpaid loans is one choice you might have for the next phase of credit recovery.

- Reducing or eliminating any or all of your debts.

- Negotiating with creditors to pay off loans in a smaller lump amount or enter into a more favorable settlement plan, preferably in return for the absence of unfavorable facts on the credit report.

- Getting help devising a strategy for paying down any or all of the loans.

- Declaring bankruptcy.

Chapter 3
Reducing Current Expenses and Debts

Figuring out ways to cut expenses and reduce current debt obligations is always smart, even if you're not in debt and your credit is good. But if you are trying to repair your credit, reducing your daily living expenses can be especially helpful.

If your living expenses and monthly debt payments are greater than your income, you may be able to turn the tables with some smart cuts and financial decisions. And even if you have enough income to cover your expenses, freeing up extra cash will allow you to employ some of the credit repair strategies discussed later in this book, paying down debt, negotiating with creditors, and even putting some money in the bank to deal with future emergencies.

CUTTING EXPENSES

Cutting your everyday life costs is an excellent way to save money. This will assist you in dealing with your creditors, who will want to know why you are unable to cover your expenses and what measures you have made to become more frugal.

Cutting costs isn't a trendy subject. Some people believe they've already cut every single corner. Some people believe that saving a few dollars here and there won't make a difference in their financial condition, so they don't see the appeal. Others believe that eliminating pleasures would render life so unbearable that it is not a viable option. Before you miss this part, think about how you feel if some of these apply to you:

- Reducing those forms of spending would not alter the way of living.

- Calculate the impact of a minor shift over the duration of a year, not just a week or a month.

- Think of what you just need to be comfortable with and just get rid of the lot. When it comes to something other than common necessities, research suggests that interactions render us happier than investments.

Here are a few cost-cutting ideas that might save you hundreds or even thousands of dollars every year.

REDUCING INSURANCE POLICY PAYMENTS

By the volume of compensation or raising the deductible, you will also save hundreds of dollars or more on the insurance premiums. It is usually more costly to have to cover minor quantities of loss (by getting a relatively modest deductible) than to pay for the harm out of pocket. Some people don't even record tiny sums because they're afraid their premiums will go up. You can save money by choosing a policy with a large premium, so be sure you can manage to cover that, either by savings or repaid credit.

It's usually simple to raise the deductible for your car, medical, dental, and homeowners' insurance policies. You will still lengthen the disability benefits delay time (which will reduce the premiums). You'll almost certainly require permission from your mortgage lender for homeowners' insurance since they don't want your property to be underinsured.

Insurance is something I'm looking at. By shopping around (at least five companies) and testing each company's discounts, you may be able to get a better deal. If you purchase more than one form of policy from the same insurer, inquire about rates, you might be eligible for a discount.

Since insurance providers want to offer higher prices to long-term clients, you will not be able to get a better deal if you've been with the same insurer for a long time. If you see a cheaper deal with another firm, see if your new insurer can match that or lower it (make sure the coverage is the same). Find out just what the fee would be if you wish to swap businesses. If your credit score isn't ideal, the bid you actually get can be lower than the one advertised.

Life insurance is an insurance that protects you from Converting a whole or universal life insurance policy (which has very high costs and a cash value, money that accumulates over time that you collect whenever you terminate the policy) into a term policy is the safest option to keep benefits while lowering fees (with low premiums and no cash value). You will let go a small portion of the current cash valuation as a transfer charge, but it may be worth it if you have a scheme that is much less expensive to sustain. However, be wary of insurance brokers who may continue to persuade you to purchase more costly insurance. Keep the phrase "term life insurance" in mind.

Another way is to use the policy's cash worth against your premiums. The usage of the cash value would be treated as a loan by the corporation. The cash benefit of your policy would not decline. However, you will be expected to refund the capital. (If you don't pay that back, the heirs' inheritance will be diminished by the sum you borrowed.) Alternatively, you may request that the cash funds be used to cover the premiums. Your currency value would be reduced, but you will not be required to refund it.

You don't need life benefits if you don't have any dependents. Save money by skipping the premium.

Other forms of security. Remove all unusual insurance plans, such as so-called limited guarantees for purchases, sudden death schemes (which only cover if you fall in an accident, which is somewhat unlikely due to most causes of death), identity theft protection, or credit card theft prevention. Many of them are prohibitively costly and have nothing in the way of advantages.

REDUCING REAL ESTATE TAXES

If your home value has decreased, have it reassessed to lower your property taxes. This could save you hundreds of dollars or more per year. Check with your local assessor or similar office to learn how to get your property reassessed.

RENT PAYMENTS

Housing payments eat up a large portion of many people's budgets. Consider whether your rent is too steep for your budget. If it is, you have several options.

Ask for a rent reduction. This might work if you live in an area where property values have declined, or the vacancy rate has increased. Check rates so you can point to comparable rentals at lower rates. Give a letter verifying the contract if the landlord wishes a rent reduction or late payments.

Make an effort to find a roommate. Based on your rental agreement, you will need to get approval from your landlord.

Change your location to one that is less expensive. Keep that in your mind that if you owe your landlord money and fail to pay, your landlord can submit the debt to national credit reporting agencies or a specialist rental background credit reporting agency. This knowledge is not provided by all landlords. However, if the landlord took legal proceedings against you, such as filing an eviction claim or suing you over debt due, you can expect it to appear in your credit records and tenant background reports.

UTILITY BILLS

Many utility providers sell discounted prices to the elderly and low-income residents, as well as emergency grants to support low-income people in covering their bills. If you have heavy heating or air conditioning costs during the winter or summer, check to see if the energy provider makes "level fees." This ensures that the annual cost is averaged over 12 months and charged in equivalent installments. True expenses are assessed against the level payments for a certain month of the year, and you are either paid for the amount outstanding or offered a rebate for any overpayment.

Contact the electric provider to inquire if you are eligible for preferential prices, level fees, or other assistance. Furthermore, charitable organizations, especially religious organizations, provide assistance to low-income individuals who need assistance with their utility bills in certain places.

The federal Weatherization Assistance Program provides assistance for low, and moderate-income families to improve the energy efficiency of their homes. By taking advantage of these programs to weatherize your home, you can reduce your utility bills and possibly increase the property value of your home. It's not always easy to find out about available weatherization services.

TELEPHONE, CABLE, AND INTERNET SERVICE

Bills for these services are notoriously high. Although all companies offer basic services at lower prices, sales agents for these companies are trained to get you into higher-priced arrangements.

Make a list of services you really need. Contact your company and ask for an explanation of each fee listed on your bill, cancel those services you don't need or can live without.

Ask about "lifeline" services, basic telephone service for a lower fee.

The government requires that telephone companies offer these services to those that qualify.

Ask about the lowest rates available (for example, basic cable or slower Internet) and bundled services (getting internet, phone, or cable from the same company.

Negotiate. If a company thinks you might cut some or all of its service, it might give you a price break. Surveys have shown that almost everyone who haggles saves money on purchases.

If you have a long-term contract for cell phone service, see "Reducing Current Debt Obligations" below for ways to reduce your monthly obligation.

ELIMINATE CREDIT CARD PAYMENT PROTECTION AND MONITORING SERVICES

Services like payment protection, identity theft protection, and credit score monitoring provide little benefit to consumers. Check your credit card agreements and cancel these services. If you feel you were misled when signing up for these services, ask for a refund.

GETTING FREE TAX RETURN PREPARATION

About 70% of Americans can have their tax returns prepared for free. Check out the following:

- Free filing. If your adjusted gross income is under a certain amount, you might qualify for a free online service to help you prepare and file your tax returns. To find out more, go to the IRS website (at www.irs.gov) and search for "Free File." Since the free online reporting is offered by private corporations, you might expect them and want and sell you other resources. Just get the free service and avoid come-ons for other services.

OTHER EXPENSES

There are many other ways to cut expenses. Most of these require some changes in your life. Here are some suggestions:

- Shrink food costs. Clip coupons, buy on sale, purchase generic brands, buy in bulk, and shop at discount outlets.

- Cut your transportation costs. Carpool, work at home, bike, take the bus or train, and combine trips. Find out if your employer offers transportation or parking discounts.

- Cut costs of cable entertainment. Discontinue cable and satellite services in favor of video streaming options, such as Roku and Amazon Fire TV.

- Make use of gardens. Discover what urban parks have to bring in terms of leisure. Taking day trips to a local state or national park instead of holidays.

- Give gifts of knowledge. Give "Get Out of Dishwashing Free" or equivalent cards to recipients, encouraging them to use them if they choose to skip a chore.

- Save big acquisitions for when they're completely important. If you really must have a car, appliance, or piece of furniture, aim to purchase it used.

- Cut out small extravagances that add up to hundreds of millions each year. Take your lunch to work; eat dinner at home; avoid purchasing high-priced coffee beverages.

- Don't owe something you won't be able to pay back, or it won't be around before the bill arrives (like shopping or meals). Instead of using credit cards, try putting aside the money you need to pay during the week.

Make a list of the ways you can save money. Mentioning your sacrifices to a trustee will help you get better terms because it shows you're sincere about keeping your debts under control.

REDUCING CURRENT DEBT OBLIGATIONS

Many people have high monthly debt payments on which they are current; that is, they have not yet missed payments or defaulted.

Reducing some of these payments (and, in some cases, eliminating them altogether) will free up cash so you can start creating a dent in your outstanding debts. And if you are having some trouble keeping your monthly obligations current, finding ways to reduce them so you can regularly make your monthly payments on time is a huge step toward repairing your credit.

REDUCE OR GET RID OF LONG-TERM CONTRACTS

Look back at Form F-10, Your Debts, for any long-term contracts you can eliminate. The fewer monthly debt obligations you have, the easier it will be for you to keep your payments current and start paying down overdue debts. For example, you may be able to cancel your cell phone contract (check first to see if there's a penalty) and get a cheaper plan, perhaps with a different carrier, or switch to prepaid phone service.

CAR PAYMENTS

Your options for reducing or eliminating car payments depend on whether you buy or lease your vehicle.

PURCHASE PAYMENTS

If a large car payment is eating up your budget, consider selling the car, paying off the lender, and using whatever is left to pay your other debts or buy a more affordable used car. This strategy may save you a bundle in car insurance payments, too.

Selling the car is not always a good strategy if you're "upside-down." However, if you can pay the difference between the loan amount and the car's market value, then selling the car will at least free up the amount of your car payment each month. Don't transfer the car to someone who promises to make the monthly payments for you, this almost certainly will violate your purchase contract. Also, if the business or person who takes the car doesn't make the payments, you'll still be responsible for the loan default, and it'll appear on your credit report.

Another option is to ask the lender to reduce the interest rate.

Or the lender might agree to rewrite the loan so that you make lower payments for the long term (you'll end up paying more interest with this option).

If you have some overdue payments but can make the monthly payments going forward, you could also ask the lender to forgo the late payments. If you are only behind by a few payments, ask if the lender will extend the loan by adding that payment to the end, which it may do for a fee. To get a good idea of what your lender may be willing to do, go to bankrate.com and search for "Keeping the auto repo man at bay."

LEASE PAYMENTS

If you can't afford your auto lease payments, consider canceling early if the penalties aren't too high. Examine the terms of your lease contract that describe what happens if you break your lease early. You should expect to pay a tax if you leave your job early.

If you can't work out how much you'll owe, write to the broker and inquire how much you'll owe if you plan to leave the contract early. Contact the leasing agent whether the dealer has already granted (sold) the contract.

If the formula that the company uses to calculate the amount you owe is not clearly defined, not included in your lease agreement, or unreasonable, you might be able to get the amount reduced or eliminate early termination penalties. You'll need a lawyer's help to do this, though. Loans for Which You Pledged Security (Other Than a Motor Vehicle) If a personal loan or store agreement is secured, for example, you pledged a refrigerator or couch as collateral for your repayment on that item, the lender probably won't agree to reduce what you owe. Instead, it may threaten to send a truck over and take the property. Keep in mind, though, that lenders rarely repossess personal property other than motor vehicles because the property value is usually not enough to make the cost of repossession worth their while. And if a creditor does come to the door to repossess an item in your home, you don't have to let the creditor in unless it has a court order.

If you propose something reasonable, however, the lender may extend your loan or rewrite it to reduce the monthly payments. However, bear in mind that you can wind up paying more in interest over time.

REDUCING MORTGAGE DEBT

If you are like many Americans, your mortgage payment may be the biggest monthly expense in your budget. After you've crunched all the numbers, you too may determine that your mortgage is just too large for your financial situation. Or, perhaps you can manage your mortgage but would love to reduce your house payments so you can use the extra money to pay off delinquent or other outstanding debts or to negotiate with creditors. Or, maybe you had a temporary financial problem that is behind you, and although you can now pay your regular mortgage payments, you can't catch up on the back payments.

Depending on your situation, reducing your mortgage debt generally involves one of these strategies:

- Getting an extension to pay back payments over time or later.

- Refinancing.

- Modifying your loan terms.

- Moving out and renting or buying a cheaper house after a sale, short sale, deed in lieu, or foreclosure.

Chapter 4
Ways to Raise Money to Pay Debts

You should have worked out how much money comes in and goes out of your home per month by now, and you should have been willing to slash any costs or reduce your existing mortgage commitments to free up more cash to go toward your debt. But there's one more thing to think about. Your financial problems can be alleviated if you can come up with extra funds per month or a lump sum of cash to pay off any of your debts. This segment addresses a few options for raising funds that you may want to explore. And if you're desperate, you shouldn't take advantage of any chance to get cash quickly. If you make a poor decision, you could end up in far more debt. As a result, pay close attention to the pages on solutions to stop.

WAYS TO RAISE MONEY

Any of the ways to explore when searching for funds to pay off the loans are mentioned below. Until taking action, weigh all of the benefits and drawbacks of each process.

GET SOME OF YOUR INCOME TAX REFUND EARLY

This choice can be useful if each month is a tight squeeze. Each month, it brings more money into your pocket. Many households have much more funds deducted from their paychecks than they would use to pay their annual income taxes. You will receive more money with each paycheck by changing the withholding to best balance your wages, rather than needing to wait for the end of the year to get a refund, by adjusting the withholding to better match your income. Request a new IRS W-4 form from the boss, or obtain one from the IRS (www.irs.gov) and complete it according to the directions or with the assistance of a tax advisor. On its website, the IRS also has a withholding calculator to assist you in determining the right sum to withhold. Go to www.irs.gov and type "withholding calculator" into the search box.

The aim is to change the withholding so that you can retain some of your earnings while paying no taxes at the end of the year. Any citizens are concerned with withholding too little and owing a substantial tax or penalty as a result. If your salary is consistent, the IRS form can change the withholding appropriately because so, if you default towards the end of the year, you are unable to owe a tax unless the underpayment is egregious. If you have some questions, seek advice from a tax professional.

You could start getting some money for the next paycheck when you return the form to your boss. (If your pay rises, remember to change your W-4 withholding accordingly.)

GET CASH BACK WITH YOUR TAX RETURN FOR LOW, AND MODERATE-INCOME FAMILIES

When you apply for an Earned Income Tax Credit (EITC), the federal government can offer you a lump amount of money after you submit your tax return. And if you aren't supposed to file a return due to your poor salary, do it anyway. This is the only way to qualify for this advantage.

Working households with low to modest incomes are eligible for the credit. An EITC is available to families of three or more children who raise up to $53,930 in the 2017 tax year. Depending on your wealth and family size, the tax refund (the equivalent of cashback to you) may be as high as $6,318. Check for "EITC" on the IRS website, www.irs.gov, to see whether you apply. When you file your federal tax form, make sure to claim the refund.

If you claimed the EITC on your tax return in 2017, the IRS would not give your refund until February 15. This covers something that isn't related to the EITC.

SELL A MAJOR ASSET

Selling a big asset, such as a vehicle, is one way to collect cash while keeping associated expenses to a minimum. If you can no longer handle the bills, this could be a good option. You'll almost certainly get more money if you sell the land yourself rather than waiting for a repossession.

You will have to pay off any outstanding debts on the estate, as well as any secured creditors to which you lent the asset as leverage, using the profits from the auction. Then you'll have to pay off whatever liens your creditors have put on the house. You will use whatever money is left to pay off the other debts. However, before you take this measure, make sure the sum you'll be clearing is worthwhile and that you have a viable alternative mode of transportation. If you don't, you'll be in much poorer shape, you won't be able to drive to work without a ride.

SELL SMALLER ITEMS

The majority of citizens have things they seldom use or no longer need. Here are some options for selling certain things and getting the money you need.

Websites for online auctions. It's never been simpler to get rid of a property you don't use, thanks to the Internet. Checking lists for related products will help you find out how much an object is worth. You will be required to pay for delivery.

WITHDRAW OR BORROW MONEY FROM A TAX-DEFERRED ACCOUNT

You can get cash to pay down loans by borrowing funds from an IRA, 401(k), or other tax-deferred savings plan until retirement, but you'll almost still have to pay the penalty and taxes. There are several disability exceptions that encourage you to take funds out of your savings account early, such as whether you become sick or have a lot of medical bills. Check the IRS magazines or online topics that contribute to the specific strategy for more details. Publication 590-B covers IRAs, while Publication 575 and IRS Topic 558 cover 401k, 403b, and 457 programs. You will be allowed to borrow funds from a 403(b), 457, or 401(k) account (instead of withdrawing it). Both choices have significant disadvantages: If you have other large savings or are genuinely exhausted, you can just suggest using either to pay off debts.

And so, this can only be seen as a final resort. Whenever possible, try to collect funds from non-retirement accounts first.

Borrowing and withdrawing money conditions vary depending on the program. Early withdrawals from a tax-deferred portfolio are costly. With a few variations (see above), any money you withdraw from your IRA, 403(b), 457, or 401(k) account before reaching the age of 59½ is considered an early distribution, and you'll owe fines and taxes on it.

Instead of removing funds, you will normally borrow up to half of your vested account balance, but not more than $50,000, via a certified scheme. Then you repay the money over a five-year period with interest. If you do not return the money within five years (or automatically if you quit the job), your "loan" will be considered as an early withdrawal, and you'll be charged an early distribution penalty as well as income tax.

CONSIDER A HOME EQUITY LOAN OR CREDIT LINE

Home equity loans (also known as "second mortgages") and home equity lines of credit (also known as "HELOCs") are available from certain banks, savings and loans, credit unions, and other lenders. Lenders who offer these loans can just lend a fraction of your equity in the market or appraised valuation of your home, usually between 50% and 80%. For instance, if the home is worth $200,000 and you owe $100,000 on it, you could be eligible for a $60,000 equity loan, bringing the gross mortgage debt to $160,000, or 80% of the house's value. When determining whether and how much to lend you, the lender would take into account your financial background, wages, and other expenditures.

There are benefits and drawbacks of taking out a home equity loan. It's almost never a smart decision to place your property in jeopardy by taking out a home equity or second mp line of credit if any of your mortgages are unsecured and your property is free from the collection. If you're late in your mortgage payments, you can talk to your lender about extending or modifying your loan.

When you opt to take out a home equity loan when you can't get a mortgage extension or expansion, or for some other excuse, make sure you fully grasp the conditions before signing on the dotted line. It's necessary that you find out how much the loan would cost you per month and whether or not you can handle it. You would more definitely sacrifice your house if you cannot buy it.

CREDIT REPAIR SECRETS

Have a look at the drawbacks and benefits of home equity loans and credit lines.

BENEFITS OF HOME EQUITY LOANS AND CREDIT LINES

- A loan of home equity allows you to borrow a certain sum of money to repay it in equivalent monthly installments for a specified period of time. You may still use a home equity line of credit (HELOC) to borrow funds as you need it, drawing on the balance you were given before you opened the account; you'll pay this sort of loan off like a credit card payment.

- You will be able to subtract all of the interest payments from your tax report.

- Home equity loans and credit lines have a number of drawbacks.

- Predatory lenders sell certain home equity loans at exorbitant interest rates. Predatory lenders prey on individuals who are in debt or who had payment troubles in the past. Predatory lenders often anticipate the borrower's inability to meet loan payments and expect to foreclose on the home (force the selling of the home) if the borrower defaults. Avoid any lender that advises you to falsify a loan application, forces you to qualify for requires you to apply for a larger loan than you need, or pressures you to take in monthly fees you can't manage, according to the Federal Trade Commission (FTC).

- Teaser prices will make a home equity loan seem more appealing than it really is. A variable interest rate on an equity loan is one that increases or falls in tandem with a specific interest rate index (sometimes referred to as an adjustable-rate mortgage or an ARM). However, the trend is usually somewhat smaller in the first six months to three years. When the original term expires, the premium immediately resets to the normal variable rate, which will result in much higher debt payments. Many citizens have recently fallen into this vortex, as loans taken out a few years ago unexpectedly become even more expensive every month, and they were unwilling or refinanced to lower their payments. If you're planning on taking out an equity loan, make sure you understand the teaser rate, whether there is one, the regular rate, when the regular rate kicks in, and how high the payments would be.

- You are committing to making a new regular or periodic bill. If you are unable to make the payments, you could be forced to sell your home or, much worse, risk eviction. Be sure you can cover the monthly cost before taking out a home equity loan.

- Interest is deductible, although it may be expensive. Instead of saving you the entire amount of interest you charged, the tax allowance helps you to exclude your interest from your revenue by calculating your income tax. The money you save from having an interest reduction is just a percentage of the interest you pay in the first instance.

- Certain loans are "interest-only" loans, which means that regular contributions only include the interest and not the principal. And if you make installments for years, you would always owe the whole sum lent.

- You have to register for an assessment, credit check, title protection, and points upfront. Thousands of dollars will be spent on these fines. In addition, certain lenders charge a yearly fee of $50 to $75 for providing you with an equity line of credit.

- When you sell the home, you must pay off the equity loan as well as any remaining mortgage debt.

- If you have a HELOC and your property's valuation drops or the creditor thinks your credit situation has gotten worse, the creditor will freeze the loan and prevent you from taking out even further money, even if you haven't borrowed the full sum allowed under the conditions of the loan.

IF YOU ARE 62 OR OLDER, YOU HAVE TO CONSIDER A REVERSE MORTGAGE

Older homeowners can access the equity in their homes through a range of plans that do not require them to travel, give up title to the land, or make debt payments. Reverse mortgages are the most popular form of plan.

Reverse mortgages are home equity loans that give borrowers cash advances that don't need redemption before the last creditor, co-borrower, or qualifying partner sells the house, moves out, or passes. A creditor may collect the funds in a variety of forms, including a lump sum, annual installments, a line of credit, or a variation of these. The debt due grows over the term of the loan when the creditor does not make payments. The homeowner maintains ownership of the house and is responsible for paying property taxes, mortgages, and maintenance expenses. The FHA's Home Equity Conversion Mortgage service is the most commonly distributed reverse mortgage program (HECM).

Reverse mortgages have seen plenty of the same characteristics as the riskiest subprime mortgages in the past. This resulted in a vast number of defaults, and when compounded with the housing bust's unparalleled drop in home prices, the FHA found itself experiencing significant losses in the past. To address this problem, new legislation enacted in 2015 strengthened the conditions for reverse mortgages funded by the Federal Housing Administration.

Before making a reverse mortgage loan, a lender may do a financial review to guarantee the applicant can pay the taxes and benefits, and the amount of funds a borrower can access in the first year is restricted. Before making a reverse mortgage, the FHA is proposing asking the investor to assess the borrower's willingness to cover the expense of services.

People who are normally 62 years old who have a variety of equity in their houses are the perfect candidates for a reverse mortgage. In certain situations, the reverse mortgage lender would base the lending decision on your maturity, the sum of equity you have in your house, and prevailing interest rates. Closing expenses (title premiums, escrow fees, and valuation fees), loan origination fees, compounded interest, mortgage insurance, annual maintenance fees, and, in most situations, an extra payment to cover the lender's risk that you won't reimburse are all charges you'll have to bear. These payments are frequently far greater than those associated with a traditional home loan. (A reverse mortgage is normally repaid by the profits from the sale of a home after the owner passes away.)

Reverse mortgages have a number of significant disadvantages. Your descendants would not be able to inherit the house until they pay off the debt until you die. Your continuing availability for need-based federal insurance services like Supplemental Social Security (SSI) and Medicaid can be impacted by a reverse mortgage.

Your freedom can be limited if you take out a reverse mortgage. When you are no longer staying in your house, the full reverse mortgage is usually due. A prolonged departure from your houses, such as a lengthy holiday, a visit to your daughters, or a stay of more than a year in an assisted living facility, could be seen by certain lenders as proof that you are no longer living in the home or haven't adequately protected it in your absence, and, as a result, that the whole debt must be paid off right away.

Another thing to keep in mind is that certain spouses have placed the reverse mortgage under the name of the older spouse just, only to find out after the older spouse's death that the whole loan was due. This effectively made the younger partner homeless.

Thanks to many legal decisions and reforms in HUD legislation surrounding the HECM scheme, a nonborrowing younger partner will also stay in the house when a reverse mortgage holder dies (and the debt redemption is postponed) if the following conditions are met:

- The reverse mortgage was approved by the Federal Housing Administration (FHA) on or around August 4, 2014.

- Other requirements are fulfilled, such as the borrower and nonborrower were married at the time the loan was closed. The debt becomes due if the non-borrowing partner fails to fulfill any of the conditions.

When the older borrowing spouse dies, the landlord may choose to assign the reverse mortgage to HUD (and the debt payoff would be deferred), allowing the younger non-borrowing spouse to stay in the house. This privilege is not guaranteed to a non-borrowing partner. And if the non-borrowing partner meets all of the qualifying requirements, the lender can opt to call the loan due and payable (and seek foreclosure) instead. The non-borrowing partner will either have to pay off the debt, sell the house, or deed it to the lender to escape foreclosure.

And if you get to keep the house, the reverse mortgage payments will end until your partner passes away. This suggests that taking out a reverse mortgage for your partner is potentially a smart decision. If the reverse mortgage is in each of your hands, you should be assured that you will be eligible to receive monthly checks or utilize an established line of credit when your partner passes away, as well as continue to remain in the house.

An annuity might be recommended by the seller or another entity in connection with a reverse mortgage. Don't fall for it. An annuity is a form of policy that is paid out of the equity of the house and starts paying the monthly creditor premiums right away.

Or after a few years, it locks up funds from a reverse mortgage for a long time, adds transaction expenses, introduces steep fines for early withdrawal, and does not help elderly homeowners (who may not survive to see their first annuity payout, whether they live that long).

There is a several-year or longer delay). Indeed, the federal government forbids lenders from requiring the procurement of an annuity from "some other entity." (12 USC 1715z-20(o)) As a prerequisite of receiving a reverse mortgage in California, lenders are prohibited from recommending homeowners to others for the acquisition of an annuity. In the end, reverse mortgages are complicated, risky, and don't always work out. Whether you're thinking about it, talk to a CPA, a financial advisor, or an elder law solicitor first.

OBTAIN A LOAN FROM A RELATIVE OR FRIEND

Some citizens are fortunate enough to have acquaintances or families who will and may assist them during a financial downturn. Remember the following when approaching your college roommate, parents, Uncle Paul, or someone else:

- Would the lender continue to assist you? You can search for a loan somewhere else if the individual is on a fixed salary and wants the funds to get by.

- Do you want to be in debt to this person? If the loan has emotional implications, make sure you can navigate the scenario before accepting the funds.

- Will the loan assist you, or will it just postpone the unavoidable (most certainly, bankruptcy)? Don't take out loans to pay down obligations that would be discharged in bankruptcy.

- Would you have to pay back the loan right away, or will the lender give you time to get back on your feet? If you have to make contributions right now, you're just introducing another monthly charge to an increasingly overwhelming debt load.

- Should you treat a loan from your parents as part of your future inheritance? If that's the case, you'll never have to pay that back. If your siblings are upset that you are having a portion of Mom and Dad's income, make sure they realize that your inheritance would be diminished as a result.

BORROW AGAINST YOUR LIFE INSURANCE POLICY

If you've got a whole life or universal life insurance policy for a while, you've most likely built up "capital value," which you will be willing to draw against. The insurance firm would ask you to repay the money lent (usually in installment payments), and if you cannot do so until you expire, the proceeds earned from your heirs will be limited by the amount owing. More information on investing against your insurance policies can be obtained from the insurance provider or the insurance firm.

OPTIONS TO AVOID

When looking for opportunities to earn funds to pay off your bills, keep in mind that there is a lot of fraud and poor offers out there. You don't want to choose a path that would exacerbate the debt problems. Here's a rundown on some of the more famous blunders to prevent while attempting to collect funds. This isn't an exhaustive collection. Every day, unfortunately, new scams and poor offers emerge. Remember that if a sale or bid sounds too nice to be real, it most likely is. If you're thinking about it, proceed with caution.

AVOID CONSOLIDATION LOANS

Consumers are lent money by certain financial firms and bank branches, mostly in the form of restructuring loans. This kind of borrowing is used to pay down any of the unpaid debts. If you take out a guaranteed consolidation loan, you'll have to put up your home, vehicle, or other valuables as security.

These loans work similarly to second mortgages or guaranteed personal loans in that you'll be paying interest ranging from 5% to more than 36%, based on the credit score and the protection. If you default on the loan, the mortgage firm has the right to seize the property you used to fund the loan, such as your house, vehicle, or other personal property.

Unsecured restructuring loans are available from finance institutions, bank branches, and other providers that can lend you money without asking you to commit any land as collateral. However, the interest rates on these loans are sometimes exorbitant, touching 35% or more. Lenders often demand a variety of penalties, all of which are hidden, taking the effective interest rate closer to 50%.

If you need a restructuring loan, you can go to a credit union or a branch rather than a bank affiliate. (Be aware that the subsidiary's name might be confusingly identical to the banks.) When you default, finance firms often partake in unethical or borderline collection activities, and they are less likely to bargain than banks and credit unions.

Consolidation loans, especially those from financial firms or related businesses (rather than credit unions or direct from banks), can be perceived negatively by prospective borrowers who see them in your credit file because they often mean previous debt issues. Furthermore, lenders that provide restructuring loans are always unable to supply you with interest rate details before you complete your applications, rendering it difficult to compare rates.

It's impossible to comparison shop without your credit background being verified. If you're thinking of getting a restructuring loan, notify the lender that even if you address any of the lender's queries, you don't want a credit inquiry or an application sent before you know the interest rate.

AVOID TAX REFUND ANTICIPATION LOANS AND CHECKS

Although having a quick tax refund is always a nice way to get cash, you can avoid taking out a refund anticipation loan or a refund anticipation review.

A RAL is a loan depending on the expected tax return from a payday lender (or any nonbank lender). RALs are therefore very costly. The Consumer Financial Protection Bureau reported in 2015 that one RAL lender charged annual percentage rates (APRs) of over 240%, while another charged APRs as much as 218%. In reality, the US military finds RALs to be predatory and bans interest rates of more than 36% for servicemembers (and their dependents) on active duty for more than a month.

RALs are not only incredibly costly, but they still face certain threats. And if the repayment is refused, delayed, or frozen, you must reimburse the loan. The lender can transfer the debt to a collection agency if you are unable to repay the loan. Unpaid debts would almost certainly show up on the credit sheet. And if you use a new loan or tax preparer next year, if you file for a RAL again, the lender will use the refund to cover this year's unpaid RAL debt.

Refund expectation tests (RACs) are sold to those who want a tax refund but can't afford to hire a tax preparer upfront. For a RAC, the tax preparer sets up a new savings account, and the IRS transfers the refund directly into it. After deducting the tax preparation fee from the refund, the residual funds are charged to you by check, and the temporary account is locked. A RAC is less costly and dangerous than a RAL, but it will not send your refund money any sooner than the IRS (unless you don't have a bank account and would wait for your refund by mail), and it will cost anything from $30 to $55. Additionally, certain tax preparers impose additional costs, such as paper printing or e-filing fees, which may vary from $25 to hundreds of dollars. If your refund is rejected or less than anticipated, you can face the same risks as if you had a RAL. Worse, several major tax planning firms persuade customers to deposit their returns on credit cards, which come with extra costs.

Rather than paying the large charge for a RAL or RAC, it is much easier to make the IRS deposit the refund into your own checking or savings account. You will usually submit your return online and get your money easily.

AVOID PAYDAY LOANS

The payday loan market is rapidly expanding. These loans are unlawful in some jurisdictions. Before you take out one of these loans, think twice.

A payday loan (also known as an advance loan by some banks) functions as follows: Either you sign an arrangement granting the lender the freedom to borrow money from your bank account or a credit card to which income, such as income, is periodically attached, or you send the lender a check to get a sum less than the face value of the check. If you send the lender a $300 post-dated check, for example, the lender will give you $250 and retain the remaining $50 as a deposit. The verification is kept by the investor for a few weeks (often until your payday). Then you would compensate the issuer the check's face value ($300), typically by authorizing the check to be cashed. If you can't cash the check, the lender will charge you another fee ($50 in this case). You owe the lender $350 at this stage (the $250 lent and the first $50 charge, and a second $50 fee). If you allow the loan access to your bank account or credit card instead of a deposit, the cost is the same. The money you borrow is paid directly into your account or card (minus the lender's fee), and the payday lender withdraws the loan until it is due. The provider would give you an extra fee if you require another loan within that week, and so on.

People that can't make good on a check wind up on a "treadmill of loans," so they have to keep signing fresh checks, or the lender allows extra withdrawals from their account to offset the penalties that have accrued, on top of repaying the money lent. According to the Pew Centre on the States, payday lenders issue an average of eight loans each year, with the average borrower spending more than $520 in interest on a $375 loan. Payday loans have astronomical average percentage rates, varying from 200% to 500% or more.

Payday loans have been a major issue for military personnel in recent years. Federal regulations cap the average percentage amount that lenders may charge servicemembers on active duty for longer than 30 days or their dependents in consumer credit extensions, including payday loans, to 36%. This ensures that a payday lender will no longer offer a servicemember more than $1.38 in interest on a two-week loan of $100. Payday lenders are often prohibited from rolling over loans to military members and their dependents because the new loans provide better conditions, such as reduced interest rates.

AVOID PAYDAY LENDER PREPAID CARDS

Prepaid cards are also offered by payday loans. The loan funds are transferred into a prepaid debit card that you can use to buy groceries, food, and other things via these services. However, as part of the loan, you must choose to deposit your potential earnings on the card.

You must also give your provider permission to deduct your debt amount from your debit card. High overdraft fees and odd costs, such as a credit for making a good payday loan payment, are common with this form of prepaid card.

AVOID PAWNSHOPS

Visiting a pawn shop could be one of the last options for obtaining funds. You leave your valuables, such as rings, a tv, or a musical instrument, at a pawnshop. In exchange, the pawnbroker can typically lend you between 25% and 60% of the item's resale value. According to the National Pawnbrokers Association, the typical pawnshop loan is just around $150.

You are granted a brief period of time to repay the loan, only a few months, and you are paid interest, which is always exorbitant. Based on what the state statute caps the prices pawnshops can offer, interest rates can range from 12% to 240% or more.

If you default on a pawnshop loan, the property you left at the shop becomes the pawnbroker's property.

AVOID AUTO TITLE PAWN OR AUTO TITLE LOANS

You borrow money toward the valuation of your paid-for car in an auto title pawn (also known as an "auto title loan" in some states). After you get the loan, you hold and operate the car, but the lender holds the title as collateral for reimbursement, as well as a backup of your keys. If you default on the loan, the lender takes possession of your car, sells it, and retains the proceeds. Any lender can pursue you for any deficiency, the difference between what you owe and what the lender was willing to recover for your vehicle. And if you just skip one bill, the landlord has the right to repossess the car. Monthly finance charges of 25% (annual interest rate of 300%) are popular. This assumes that if you borrow $500 for a month, you'll have to pay $125 in interest and any extra fees the lender needs, according to the FTC.

Military personnel used to be a popular option for auto title lending companies. However, lenders are unable to offer auto title loans to military personnel owing to new amendments in federal legislation.

AVOID PEER-TO-PEER LOANS

P2P crowdfunding platforms like Lending Club and Prosper encourage you to borrow up to $40,000 from "ordinary citizens" to consolidate loans or pay off credit cards, for example. P2P lending's biggest selling point is that it often provides lower rates than conventional bank rates, often as low as 6% to 7%. However, the low rating is only available to anyone with excellent credit ratings. Many with poor reputations won't be eligible (you'll need a credit score in the 600s to even get a P2P loan by Lending Club or Prosper), and riskier borrowers would pay much higher interest rates if approved (up to around 25% to 35%). Furthermore, there are charges associated with this kind of operation. There's an origination charge (around 1% to 5%) just to receive the loan, plus you'll usually have to add a check processing fee if you pay via check. You'll be paid a fee whether you're late for the deposit or it bounces, typically $15 or 5% of the loan, whatever is higher, for late payment and $15 for a bounced payment.

AVOID EASY SOLUTIONS TO DEBT PROBLEMS OFFERED ON TV OR THE INTERNET

Keep an eye out for advertisements on tv, radio, the Internet, or direct mail that promise simple debt remedies. You will not always be able to say what these firms are selling.

ADVERTISEMENTS FOR DEBT CONSOLIDATION LOANS

Any advertisements could be for costly consolidation loans that you can avoid because they have excessive interest rates, secret costs, and protection provisions that place your existing property at risk.

ADS FOR UNLICENSED BANKRUPTCY ASSISTANCE

Other ads tout the services of unlicensed people claiming they can eliminate your debts through bankruptcy; often, these services file incorrectly or don't follow through, which makes it harder for you to get bankruptcy relief if you need it.

ADS FOR DEBT RELIEF SERVICES

Many advertisements that want to help you get out of debt are simply advertisements for debt management programs. These businesses advertise debt collection, arbitration, pooling, settlement, and prorating as services. They pretend to be willing to get borrowers to pay even less than you owe, but what they do is demand large rates to take the money and transfer it to your creditors, which you will do yourself.

CHAPTER 5
WAYS TO IMPROVE YOUR CREDIT HISTORY

Here are some ways to improve your credit history and score without getting new credit.

OPEN DEPOSIT ACCOUNTS

Nine out of ten American adults have checking accounts, those who do tend to weather financial problems better and save more. Bank accounts are used as a symbol of prosperity among creditors. To be honest, they often search at bank accounts to ensure that you can cover the bills.

A deposit or money market account can also help you increase your credit score. Creditors believe that individuals who have investment or money market accounts use them, even though they never invest additional money into them. Using a bank account ensures two points to creditors: You're saving money because if you don't pay the bill and the creditor has to prosecute you to recover, the creditor would have a source on which to collect the verdict. Getting an account would also enable you to set money aside for costs that occur on a daily basis during the year.

You shouldn't be refused a bank account only because you have a bad credit background. If you have a poor check-writing background, you will be refused an account. Before opening an account for you, most banks can verify your check-writing background through a check verification firm. If you're refused a bank account due to evidence submitted by a check verification firm, ask the bank for the company's contact information. To obtain a copy of your credit report, contact the firm. If you can't settle the issue informally, you can appeal missing or incorrect records in the company's files through a dispute note, much as you can with a credit reporting service.

HIGH RISK   **MEDIUM RISK**   **LOW RISK**

SHOPPING FOR AND CHOOSING A BANK ACCOUNT

You must shop around to find the best account for you. A 2012 Pew Research survey of the 12 largest banks and 12 largest credit unions found that banks and credit unions charged anywhere from 4 to 48 separate fees on checking accounts. The kinds and amounts of fees varied dramatically among these institutions. If you are not careful, you could end up with an account that actually makes repairing your credit harder because of excessive and hidden fees.

Credit unions and local community banks often have lower checking or saving account fees and require less money to open an account than do large national banks. According to www.bankrate.com, 72% of credit unions don't charge monthly maintenance fees for checking accounts, whereas only 38% of bank checking accounts are free. The average monthly fee for large banks is typically around $10 to $12, but sometimes you don't have to pay the fee by maintaining a minimum balance, setting up direct deposit, or using self-service banking instead of coming into the branch. Credit unions are often a good place to start getting credit when you are ready for that.

Many banks scatter the important information you need to compare fees among, on average, nearly 70 pages of information, according to the survey. Credit unions use fewer than half as many pages, on average, but this is still a lot to search through. A 2014 follow-up to the earlier Pew survey found that many banks are now offering better disclosures about account fees. However, often not all fees are disclosed on a bank's or credit union's website, so you have to go to a branch to get all the necessary information.

To comparison shop successfully, make a checklist of the important fees and costs so you can compare the information you get from different banks and credit unions. Compare at least these features:

- The amount you need to open an account.

- The monthly fee.

- Whether the bank supplies checks for free, and if not, the cost of checks.

- How you can avoid the monthly fee (usually by directly depositing your regular income check or keeping a high balance).

- The fee for writing a check without sufficient funds (NSF fee).

- Overdraft fees (these are charged if the bank cashes your check and you don't have enough in your account to cover it), including fees for transferring the money from another account or credit card or any additional fees, tacked on for additional days while your account is overdrawn.

- The maximum number of overdrafts the bank will process in a day.

- The order in which the bank will post checks.

- The interest rate, if any, is paid on the account.

- ATM fees at that bank's branches and at other banks' ATM machines.

- All other fees (for example, a returned mail fee, closing an account early fee, or fees for using a human teller).

Then compare fees for several credit unions and banks. You can find this information for some banks on websites like www.bankrate.com. You can get information from local credit unions and community banks by reviewing their websites or visiting a nearby branch.

Once you have all the information, choose an account that works with the way you'll use it.

If you often use ATMs, for example, search for a bank or credit union that waives ATM fees and reimburses you for fees charged by other banks. Also, do not authorize overdrafts or overdraft protection because it can cause you to pay high fees for overdrafts or for the overdraft protection service.

AVOID BOUNCING CHECKS

If you open a banking account, avoid bounced checks at all costs. Check 21 is a statutory statute that requires banks to process electronic images of checks rather than physical originals. As a consequence, checks clear even more quickly than in the past. To avoid bouncing checks, don't write a check unless you know the funds are already in the account to cover it. Although checking account information is not included in credit reports prepared by the three nationwide credit reporting agencies, if you bounce a check to a creditor, it most likely will report a late or missed payment to a credit reporting agency, jeopardizing your hard work to repair your credit. Bounced check background may make it more difficult to open bank accounts in the future.

USE YOUR CREDIT CARDS WISELY

Whether you have a cash card, a department store card, or a fuel card that has a grace period, use that to settle your bills on time if you have suffered a financial crisis. Your credit score would easily increase. Payment records over the last two or four years are typically seen on credit reports. Your credit report would reflect steady and proper usage of revolving credit if you owe anything every month or so, no matter how little, and pay it off during the grace period (usually 21 days or so after you collect the bill).

ASK TO INCREASE YOUR CREDIT LIMIT

Your credit history will improve if you use less of the credit that is available to you. In fact, some experts recommend you never charge more than a third to one-half of the limit on your credit cards. One way to change your ratio of debt to available credit is to ask your creditors to increase your credit limits on existing cards (if you have any). This will immediately cause your outstanding credit card debt to become a smaller percentage of your credit limit. Of course, for this to work, your outstanding balance must remain the same, which means you can't use the credit limit increase as an excuse to charge more.

To improve your chances of getting an increased credit limit, ask for the increase after you have brought any delinquencies current, made your monthly payments on time for several months or more, and already reduced the outstanding balance somewhat by paying more than the minimum payment each month. Creditors on accounts you have had for a long time are probably more likely to increase your credit limit than creditors on newer accounts. If the creditor denies your request, you can get more information about its decision.

An advantage of requesting a credit limit increase over applying for new credit is that it might not show up as an inquiry in your credit report. Credit reporting agencies may treat information requests by one of your existing creditors as a creditor's normal monitoring of its credit accounts rather than as a credit inquiry.

CONSIDER CLOSING CREDIT CARD ACCOUNTS

Should you close credit card accounts as a way to improve your credit score? Closing an account would not exclude any derogatory details from your credit report. Other explanations for closing credit card accounts can exist, though.

CLOSE OR KEEP YOUR ACCOUNT? HOW TO DECIDE?

Here are some points of consideration when deciding whether to close an account or keep it open.

Reasons to close credit card accounts. Creditors may be concerned if you have too many credit cards. (See "How Many Credit Cards Should You Carry?" below.) Limiting your credit accounts can also simplify your efforts to keep on top of your debt payments. Some studies show that consumers spend more if they use credit cards than if they pay in cash. Often, certain credit cards have no time limit or have such high fees and interest rates that you might want to shutter them before accruing any further fees and charges. You can also reduce the risk of loss or theft of credit cards by limiting the number you carry.

It just like that if you were delinquent on an account and couldn't bring it current or negotiate a settlement, you were better off closing the account yourself before the creditor did. Now, however, Experian says it doesn't matter who closed the account, you or the creditor. But others still recommend that you make sure your credit report reflects that you (not the creditor) closed the account.

Reasons to keep credit card accounts open. If you have an account with a high credit limit and no or only a low balance, closing the account will reduce your total credit limit, which can lower your credit score.

Even if you close a card on which you have a high balance if the card is not maxed out, closing it could lower your score. And if you have had the account for a very long time, closing it will decrease the average time of your credit history, which also lowers your credit score.

The third option: Keep the card but don't use it. If you think closing a credit card will negatively impact your credit history (perhaps because it has no balance or a low balance, or you have had it a long time), and the card doesn't have any fees that apply unless you use it, consider keeping the account open, but stop using the card. Use it seldom, and pay it off during the grace period before interest is added. (If you never use the card, eventually, the creditor will close the account for non-use.) If it has an outstanding balance, work at paying off the balance, but don't use it for additional purchases or cash advances.

Closing accounts. When you plan to terminate an account, you will do it even if the balance isn't paid off. Your account will be closed, and your rights will be revoked by the card issuer. It will give you a bill for the unpaid balance or financial statements before the balance is paid off. Alternatively, call the bank whose card you want to hold to request that the balance on the account you are closing be transferred to an account you want to keep.

Here are several other ways to determine which card accounts to close if you decide to close some but not all:

- Close the accounts with the biggest monthly payments if you pay the bill in full per month, that is if you don't hold a debt.
- If you have a reserve, close the accounts with the maximum interest rates and shortest grace periods; if you have a

balance, close the accounts with the highest interest rates and shortest grace periods. Also, read the disclosures about the credit card companies' billing practices. How interest is calculated may make a big difference in how much interest you pay, even when different accounts charge the same interest rate.

HOW TO CLOSE A CREDIT CARD ACCOUNT

If you wish to close a credit card account properly, then do it in the right way. If you pay some bills through automatic deduction from your credit cards, such as gym dues or video streaming fees, cancel those billing arrangements before closing your account. Then notify the credit card issuer that you want a "hard tight." If you don't do this, the organization can offer you a "soft close," which ensures new charges will go through despite the fact that you requested the account be closed. You are vulnerable to credit card theft if you use a soft near. If a creditor refuses to do a hard close until a certain amount of time has passed, demand that it does a hard close at that later date and send you a letter when it does.

Also, request, in writing, that the credit card company report to the credit reporting agencies that your account was "closed by consumer request" and get written confirmation that it did so. Potential creditors can look down on accounts that are incorrectly stated as "closed by creditor." Check the credit report every 30 days to make sure that the account in dispute was "closed by customer order."

AVOID DEBIT CARDS

Debit cards, some people say, are a safer choice than credit cards since they will help you manage your expenses. Does this imply that debit cards are a decent value for money? No, it's not true. Since the federal Electronic Funds Transfer Act (15 U.S.C. 1693; 12 C.F.R. 1005 and following) protects those who use debit and ATM cards, it also leaves a number of loopholes that can save you a lot of money. Privacy rights and consumer protection advocates recommend against using debit cards.

Here's why.

No grace periods. For a debit card, money is deducted from your account nearly instantly.

There is no warranty on faulty sales. If you have a difference of opinions with a retailer or another vendor about a product or service you purchased with a debit card, there is no way to dispute the charge or make an argument or defense that the product or service was not as advertised, faulty, or never delivered, unlike with credit cards.

Less protection for lost or stolen cards or unauthorized transfers. If you report the loss or theft of your debit card within two business days after you discover it, your maximum loss is $50. But if you don't report it within that time period, you could lose up to $500. If you let 60 days go by, your loss could be unlimited.

Fees and notification of conditions changes. The types and amounts of fees that banks may charge for debit cards are unrestricted. If the bank raises rates or restricts your rights, you just get a 21-day warning, often fewer.

Theft is a serious crime. Debit cards, according to reports, are more vulnerable to fraud than credit cards.

Fees on overdrafts. If you're going to retain your debit card, considering the drawbacks, don't sign up for overdraft security. The potential humiliation of a transaction being denied while your account is zero is well worth the money saved by preventing overdraft fees. Banks will charge overdraft fees for checks and frequently scheduled debits that you have approved even though you don't opt into overdraft security (for example, when you authorize a utility company to automatically debit your account each month).

No benefit for your credit history. If you are trying to re-establish or establish good credit, a debit card won't help you.

Somehow you do get a debit card, treat it like a checking account. Use a check register to record each debit transaction and calculate the balance left in your account. If the bank offers online banking, check your account frequently. Otherwise, you won't know when you have reached the limit in your bank account.

AVOID PREPAID CARDS

Prepaid cards are rechargeable cards that can be used to make payments. The cards are sold at various stores and major retailers and offered by such businesses as tax preparation companies to pay your tax refund. With some, you can even have your wages loaded on the card. These look like debit cards and usually have a bank or credit card name brand, but these cards are not linked to the account of your bank.

The major downside to prepaid cards is that they're loaded with monthly fees, activation fees, cash fees, customer service fees, overdraft fees, and more. In fact, the fees might end up costing you more than a credit card with a very high interest rate.

Another negative is that prepaid cards currently lack the protections that come with debit or credit cards. However, this could change soon. The rules will strengthen cardholder rights and make prepaid cards more consumer-friendly (although a delay in the effective date has been proposed). Among other things, the CFPB rules will require financial institutions to:

- Provide certain disclosures before you get the card.
- Limit your losses if the card is stolen or lost.
- Investigate and resolve errors.
- Provide you with free and convenient access to your account information.

BUILD CREDIT IN YOUR OWN NAME

If you're married, separated, or separating, and the majority of your credit is in the name of your partner or ex-spouse, you can consider applying for credit in your own name.

Obtaining loans under your own name is often a good way to restore your credit in the following situations:

Your partner is to blame for any or much of your financial issues.

- You and your partner have shared financial challenges together, but the majority of your credit is in your spouse's name only.

Credit reporting agencies cannot include information about your spouse's accounts on your credit report unless it's a joint account, you are permitted to use the account (for example, you are an authorized user on the account), or you are otherwise responsible for payment on the account (for example, because you guaranteed or co-signed a loan, and for most debts during a marriage in a community property state). Honestly speaking, this means that many of your spouse's credit accounts will appear in your credit history. If your spouse's credit is good, having those accounts show up in your credit history is good for you. If they don't appear in your credit history, have them added. On the other hand, if your spouse's credit is poor, you want creditors to know if you were not responsible for those accounts.

If you are divorced or separated, and most of the loans and credit cards you acquired during the marriage were in your spouse's name only, you won't have a lengthy history of good credit in your report. Here are the steps to take to start building good credit in your own name.

REQUEST THAT ALL ACCOUNTS BE INCLUDED IN YOUR CREDIT HISTORY

If you are still married and the accounts are in good standing, you can start by making sure that all joint accounts, accounts you are permitted to use and accounts that you are obligated to pay to appear on your credit report, too. If you are divorced, you can still make sure that those accounts were reported under your name for the time period during your marriage.

Identify the joint accounts and accounts on which you are responsible for paying, or you are permitted to use that you want to have added to your credit history. If you are divorced, identify the time period to which your request applies. In addition to the general rules requiring credit reporting agencies to reinvestigate your dispute, the Equal Credit Opportunity Act (ECOA) requires credit reporting agencies to add those accounts to your credit history within 90 days of your written request. (12 C.F.R. § 1002.10(a)(1).) Be sure to document your request. Ask Creditors to Consider Your Spouse's Credit History Although a credit reporting agency cannot include information about your spouse's positive credit accounts on your credit report (except for joint accounts and accounts you are permitted to use or obliged to pay) if you are applying for a loan, a credit card, or another kind of credit; you can always ask the creditor to consider any of your spouse's or former spouse's accounts that accurately reflect favorably on your creditworthiness, too. For example, if you and your former spouse made payments on your spouse's account with joint checks, provide the creditor copies of the joint account checks. If a creditor considers credit histories in making its credit decisions, the ECOA requires a creditor to consider the information you present about your spouse's or former spouse's accounts that accurately reflects your creditworthiness.

ASK CREDITORS NOT TO CONSIDER YOUR SPOUSE'S CREDIT HISTORY

If your spouse caused credit problems on joint accounts or on accounts you were permitted to use or responsible for paying; you can present information to a potential creditor to show why the account does not reflect your creditworthiness. For example, if you were unemployed, but you could not ensure that your spouse, who was working, paid the bills, you could provide documentation to show the creditor why the poor credit history should not be attributed to you. Or, if you were only a genuine user and were not responsible under the credit agreement (or under state law, such as with community property laws) to pay on the account, you could present that information to the creditor. If the creditor considers credit histories in making its credit decisions, the ECOA requires the creditor to consider the information you present.

Chapter 6
Choosing Credit Cards

You'll probably have a credit card for a long time if you have one, so choose carefully to receive the best terms possible.

COMPARISON SHOPPING: WHAT TO LOOK FOR IN A CREDIT CARD

Do some comparison shopping while applying for a new credit card to find the best value available. Credit card terminology and interest rates differ, and these differences will have a significant impact on your pocket. Since credit card issuers are required to post details about their credit cards on their websites, comparison shopping is also simpler than ever.

CONSIDER THE FOLLOWING WHEN LOOKING FOR A CREDIT CARD

Fast interest rates can be avoided. Examine the yearly percentage rate (APR). Often credit cards have a variable interest rate, which fluctuates based on an index rate. Others charge a certain fee. If you can have a set amount, you'll know how high the bills will be in the future. In addition, certain cards have separate APRs with different balances. Purchases, for example, have the lowest APR, whereas cash advances have a higher APR. Few credit card firms give a low initial APR on a balance transfer to entice you to transfer money from another credit card but still raise the payment a few months later. Examine the fees charged by the firm on any of these APRs. When shopping for a credit card, aim for the one with the lowest and most stable APR. If you bear a debt from month to month, even a minor change in the APR will have a significant impact on the amount you spend over the course of a year.

Low introductory prices can be avoided. Some credit cards have low introductory rates (also known as promo rates) that increase dramatically after a few months. Furthermore, advertised prices can extend only to individuals, such as those with a high income or a good credit score.

Find out if there is an APR strike. Late fees on most credit cards result in a hefty fee and a fresh, even higher interest rate, known as a penalty APR. These percentages may be as big as 30%. In addition, if you are late on payments to another borrower, a credit card issuer may increase the interest rate on potential purchases. Look at the deal to see what would result in a penalty APR.

Examine the grace time. This is the interest-free period that runs from the date of the sale until the due date. You don't want a credit card with no grace date.

Avoid paying exorbitant annual rates. You like a card with no monthly charge if you pay off the balance every month. If you have a debt, a card with a low annual charge and a low-interest rate could be preferable to one with no annual fee but a high interest rate if you carry a balance. Any cards with no monthly fee waive the cost for a short period or if you pay a minimum sum.

Keep an eye out for hidden costs. In addition to the interest rate, several credit card firms charge a range of processing fees for items like cash advances, and balance changes are two types of cash advances. Credit cap increases, setup costs, and returned object fees are also fees that certain cards charge.

Recognize the techniques for calculating balances. The credit card issuer calculates the finance fee for the month by applying the APR to the card balance. New acquisitions may or may not be included in the balance. It's preferable that it excludes new sales so the balance would be smaller, and the rate of interest you pay would be lower as well.

The balance is usually determined in one of the following ways:

- Daily balance method. Per day, the corporation adds fresh sales and subtracts contributions made to the starting balance. The corporation estimates the financing fee for each day's balance and applies the numbers to get the total finance expense for the billing period.

- Adjusted balance method. This is the right strategy for you. The credit card issuer subtracts all charges received during the billing period from the balance you are owing at the outset of the billing cycle. Purchases made recently are not included.

- Previous balance method. The financing fee is calculated using the balance you are owing at the start of the payment period. It does not have any charges made during the billing period.

- Average daily balance method. Your balances are added on each day in the billing period and then divided by the number of days in the cycle. The everyday sums you owe are calculated by subtracting payments made over time. Depending on the plan, new sales will or may not be covered.

- Know the credit limit. The credit cap is the maximum sum you can spend on your credit card for payments, cash advances, balance changes, fines, and finance costs combined. The credit cap isn't required to be disclosed in credit card deals, and certain creditors don't even report that when you request. Check the credit balance on a new card before activating or using it. If it's too poor to be helpful, write a letter requesting a clarification (Form F-32, Request for Basis of Unfavorable Credit Offer or Action) and suggest canceling the card before using it. Since your credit limit is limited, maxing out your credit card is an easy way to lower your credit score.

- Avoid over-limit protection and over-limit fees. Creditors can make a strong effort to get you to join over-limit insurance plans or accept over-limit charges (and the accompanying high fees). It's not a good idea. This is a quick way to re-enter the debt cycle. Be sure you don't consent to these charges by mistake. Are you unsure that you "agreed"? You must get a signed letter from the organization stating your arrangement. Since you agreed, you have the right to cancel it at any moment. (Over-limit fees will only extend on purchases that have already been processed.)

- Evaluate rebates, free miles, and other perks. Through using a credit card, you can collect cashback, free airline miles, savings on food among services, charitable donations, and other benefits. Consider the other card terms before signing up for a card dependent solely on these benefits. You are best off without the benefits if you are willing to accept heavy interest and annual rates.

- Beware of deferred credit offers by stores. Stores occasionally run deals on credit cards that guarantee "no interest if charged in full in xx days." If you do not pay off the whole balance before the end of the grace period, the card retailer may charge interest on the whole sum from the day you made the payment (usually at a high rate). So, if you buy a stove for $500 and just pay $400 at the end of the no-interest era, the shop has the right to charge you interest from the day you bought the stove. It gets trickier if the card you're using to allow the "no-interest" buy still has a balance on it. Your contributions would not actually go toward the no-interest purchase in any scenario.

- Shop for terms that work best for you. The right words for you can be determined by how you plan to use your passport. As a general rule, opt for a card with no annual charge and a lengthy grace period if you are certain you can still settle your monthly payment in full and don't worry about benefits like free miles. If you plan to bring a balance from month to month or will need to in the future (for example, to cope with a work loss or medical emergency), check for a card with a low yearly percentage rate (APR).

- Tips for shopping online. Credit card companies are required by federal legislation to post their agreements online. Check for "disclosures" or "terms and conditions" links on the credit card company's website (sometimes they are small and obscure). You'll even notice a sample arrangement under these words.

GETTING INFORMATION ABOUT CREDIT CARD TERMS AND RATES

Knowing you can compare stores, particularly for the APR, is one thing; actually, having details about the words you care about is another. "The regular APR would be 7.99% to 17.99% depending on your creditworthiness as you open your account," says one credit card deal on the Internet.

You may still apply for a few cards and see what the conditions are like, so the inquiries would show up on your credit sheet. Not every situation is perfect.

Here are few ideas to help your comparison shopping:

Don't be concerned with credit inquiries. Just 10% of the FICO credit score is made up of inquiries and fresh credit. According to FICO, most people's FICO ratings would be affected by a single inquiry by less than 5 points. So, if getting details regarding the conditions requires registering for a passport, go ahead and do that. Check the conditions carefully if you are accepted.

- Be aware of your credit report. To get a rough idea of your credit score, go to www.bankrate.com and use the FICO estimator.

- Take advantage of online credit card comparison polls. Bankrate.com, for example, compares the conditions of several credit cards. The surveys would not provide any of the relevant options or any of the terms.

- Get the full "terms and conditions" from the company's website if you find a card that looks promising.

- Consult your local banks or credit unions for more details. They may have better terminology than the ones you will find on the internet.

- Look over Consumer Reports' credit card advice. Reviews can be found online, or the magazine can be obtained at the local library.

- Speak with executives from credit card companies. Before you fill out an online questionnaire, do this. Inquire about your situation's potential APRs and credit caps.

BEWARE OF PREAPPROVED CREDIT CARD OFFERS

If you have opted out, you would most likely get credit card deals in the mail. These deals will range from decent to poor, to absolutely ugly. Any of the forms mentioned below should be avoided.

Preapproved deals that seem to be too nice to be true. Preapproved coupons for department stores, gasoline, and certain debit cards are infamous for implying low-interest rates and large credit caps in their offers, just to provide you with low credit limits, high-interest rates, and penalties, arguing that your credit background did not deserve better conditions.

Nonbank payment preapproval solicitations. A "gold" or "platinum" card with a large credit limit could be nothing more than a card that enables you to buy products from the company's catalogs. These cards are not accepted by any other retailer, and the organization will not disclose the charges and payments to credit bureaus. "The Lowdown on So-Called Gold, Platinum, and Pre-Approved Credit Cards" is a good place to start.

USING CREDIT CARDS: HOW TO PROTECT YOURSELF

To stop getting into credit card debt or being a target of credit card theft, take care when using your credit card after you've picked a decent one.

TIPS FOR SAFE CREDIT CARD USE

When you have a credit card, do the following:

- Give your creditors a change of address notice when you pass.
- If you need a credit limit boost, request it.
- Keep your cards secure. As soon as your cards come, sign them. If you have a personal identification number (PIN) for cash advances, memorize it rather than writing it down near your credit card. Have a record of your credit card issuers, account details, and phone numbers so you can contact them immediately if your card is missing or stolen.
- Never let out your credit card or bank account number on the phone unless you initiated the call and feel confident in the company's credibility.
- Take precautions to avoid identity fraud.

REVIEW YOUR CREDIT CARD STATEMENT AND OTHER NOTICES

The credit card issuer will give you notes, either individually or through your bill, reminding you of any modifications to the conditions and outlining your privileges. Keep an eye out for and read these notes.

Each month, check your account to see how much you've invested in fees and interest. You will maintain more track of your expenses if you pay attention to these figures, and you can determine if you can get a new credit card for reduced payments or interest if you do.

Check the following detail on your financial statement whether you have an unpaid balance or are in credit card debt trouble:

- How much time is required to pay off the balance, and how much it would be if you just make the minimum payments.

- The sum you'd have to spend to pay down your debt in three years or fewer.

- How much money would you save if you paid down the debt in three years rather than now making the minimum payment?

Finally, closely examine the credit card records for mistakes and fraudulent payments. Payment insurance, identity fraud protection, and credit report management are both services that millions of Americans are unknowingly paying for. Since the subscription payments are too low, it's possible to miss these services.

CHAPTER 7
HOW TO PROTECT YOURSELF?

You must take great care of your personal details. Here are few pointers about how to keep your personal details safe:

- Don't take your Social Security number, birth certificate, or visa around with you all the time.
- Don't put incoming bill deposits in your mailbox for the postal carrier to collect.

Change your passwords and PIN numbers frequently. Don't use obvious codes such as consecutive numbers, birthdays, or the names of your spouse, children, or pets. Choose a phrase you will remember and use the first letter of each word, substituting numbers for certain letters and using some capital letters.

- Examine your credit card receipts, as well as your phone and energy bills, for any transactions you didn't approve.
- Once in a year, obtain a copy of all of the credit reports. (You can calendar your requests to stagger them, so you get a report from one of the three nationwide credit reporting agencies every four months.) Promptly challenge any

inaccurate information.

- Periodically check with the three nationwide credit reporting agencies to be sure an identity thief has not used your child's Social Security number or other personal information to get credit.

- Carry your debit card, credit card, and ATM receipts with you at all times, and never throw them out in public.

- Rip or tear up all documents containing confidential details, as well as any sales of previously approved credit cards you don't want to use. Also, be wary of deals from firms you're unfamiliar with. If you have your Social Security number, mother's maiden name, and signature, it's simple to build an official-looking and totally fake credit application giving you preapproved credit.

- Be sure your financial documents, credit cards, and other confidential documents are kept in closed drawers or cabinets if you have folks working in your house.

- Invest in a shredder and use it often.

- Only send personal details on the phone if it is absolutely appropriate, and only if the call was made by you.

- If you don't know the author of an email, don't open it.

- Someone who asks about a Social Security number can be avoided. Try moving the business somewhere if a corporation refuses to conclude a contract without it.

- Be wary of demands for personal details from what seems to be a consulting firm, a corporation, or a financial entity in which you do business. Customers are seldom contacted for this reason by legitimate companies. Any such appeal, whether made over the phone or online, is almost certainly from a scammer looking to steal your sensitive details. Phishing is a kind of online fraud in which you are tricked into handing out personal or financial information by receiving spam emails or pop-up alerts. The letter purports to be from a firm with which you do business and directs you to a phony website that claims to be legitimate. The Federal Trade Commission warns against reacting to these communications by clicking on the given reply button or connection. Instead, contact the firm from a number you believe is valid, or open a new browser tab and go to the firm's right website address. The relation cannot be copied and pasted into the post.

- If you receive a "Move Validation Letter" from the post office, and you aren't moving, call the toll-free number in the letter to alert the post office. Someone may be trying to set up a fake address to open new accounts using your name.

- Contact the firm to see how the documents were compromised if you get a note about a data breach (or read of it in the news). A data breach occurs when someone breaks through or hacks into a company's database logs, and the personal details might have been compromised. When you receive correspondence from an organization that has had a data breach that might have compromised your accounts, notify the company immediately using the contact details included on the daily bills or account statements to ensure that the notification is genuine. Find out what sort of data was snatched. If it was just the credit card details that were stolen, keep an eye on certain reports and make sure no fraudulent charges are added. Alternatively, you or the organization can determine that canceling the credit card number and getting a new one is preferable. If your debit card was compromised by the hack, you could cancel it immediately. Place a fraud notice on your credit file if your Social Security number has been compromised. For more details, see the paragraph below titled "If Your Identity Is Stolen."

- Rather than have the latest checks sent to you, pick them up at the store. Your Social Security or driver's license number should not be written on your checks.

- Put no personal details on your computer home page, online internet profile, or social network websites, such as your mother's maiden name, birth date, pet's name, or any distinguishing personal information. In Internet transfers, provide as little credit and personal details as possible. If the web isn't safe, don't give out personal or financial details.

- If you get your personal information somewhere on the Internet, demand that it be removed.

OPTING OUT OF INFORMATION SHARING

It's also crucial to understand what relates to the personal data you provide to businesses, advertisers, and government departments. These organizations can use or distribute your personal details in order to support their own products and services.

Many other businesses and organizations encourage you to opt out of getting the details exchanged with others or used for advertising purposes, and financial services are allowed to do so. By opting out, you will hold more of your personal details confidential and make yourself less prone to identity fraud. Consumers who care for their privacy read the "privacy alerts" that companies give them as they open accounts. These customers want not to have their sensitive details used in the way the company's privacy policy allows. Doing this reduces the distribution of the consumers' personal information somewhat and also cuts down the number of offers and solicitations that the consumers receive.

You may also need to take steps to reduce your junk mail so that fewer sources of information about you are available in your mailbox or trash bin or are sold to other companies.

SECURITY FREEZES

In your credit file, you may even place a "security freeze" or "file freeze." A protection freeze is a note in your file that prevents the credit rating firm from disclosing your credit report or any details included in it to potential creditors without your permission. You will "unfreeze" the file with a particular borrower or for a specific duration of time (when applying for new credit).

Security freezes are available by law in all states, although sometimes the law only applies in cases of identity theft. Limits on fees credit reporting agencies may charge for placing a security freeze on your file vary by state; in some states, there is no charge if you have been a victim of identity theft. Currently, the three nationwide credit reporting agencies also voluntarily provide security freezes to all consumers even if state law does not require it.

You should carefully weigh the disadvantages and advantages of a protection freeze. They are favored by consumer advocates, especially if you are concerned about or have been a target of identity theft. You can usually lift the freeze in a few minutes by telephone, mail, or online. If you do put in place a security freeze, be sure to lift it temporarily in advance of applying for credit because it may take up to a few days to lift the freeze. Check each of the nationwide credit reporting agencies' websites for details.

PROTECTING YOUR SOCIAL SECURITY NUMBER

One approach to reducing the chance of identity fraud is to be very cautious when disclosing your Social Security number (SSN). Many citizens believe they must give their Social Security number to banks or government agencies that request it. However, this isn't necessarily the case; in certain situations, you aren't required to show it. Although, you must provide your SSN for employment, banking, real estate transactions, and many credit transactions.

If a government agency asks for your Social Security number, they must inform you if giving it is required or optional. Providing the SSN is required by several government bodies, including tax officials, welfare offices, and government agencies of motor vehicles, but not always. Whether it isn't, the government can't refuse you a reward or program because you won't reveal your Social Security number.

Employers, and even most banks, will demand that you reveal your Social Security number. Other private companies, on the other hand, are normally not allowed to ask for the SSN. Few companies have a valid excuse to ask for your phone number (for example, as you request for credit), although it's often used for record-keeping purposes in other ways. You don't have to offer your Social Security number to a company simply because it asks for it. Before you made up a decision on whether or not to send out your phone number, consider the following:

- Why do you require my phone number?

- What would my phone number be used for?

- Is there any rule that allows me to send you my phone number?

- What if I don't offer you my phone number?

- Can I send you an identifying number other than my Social Security number, or only the last four numbers of my SSN (Social Security number)?

- Is it possible to set up my account, so that I can use anything other than my SSN as an identification (for example, a mixture of letters from my last name and numbers)?

You should leave the space vacant or write "refused" if you don't want to use your SSN while filling out a request.

However, if you don't have your SSN, a business can decline to service you. In certain cases, you might choose to reveal the phone number to prevent further complications. You might choose to move the company somewhere in other cases.

Check your Social Security salary and pension declaration once a year to make sure no one else is utilizing your Social Security number for jobs. The Social Security Administration started mailing paper statements to employees aged 25, 30, 35, 40, 45, 50, 55, and 60 who do not receive Social Security payments and have not applied with an online account as of September 2014. (The Social Security Administration used to mail the benefits statements each year but stopped in 2011 due to budget cuts.) As of 2017, statements will be sent only to people who are 60 and older who haven't established an online account. To check yours annually online, go to www.socialsecurity.gov/myaccount.

If your SSN (Social Security number) is being used for jobs by someone else, call the Social Security Administration's abuse hotline (800-269-0271) right away. Try having a fresh SSN if you've ever been a target of identity fraud. This isn't going to be quick. Only if you can prove that you've taken no such measures to address the identity fraud and are not being harmed by the abuse of your Social Security number can the Social Security Administration amend your status. Even if you meet the criteria, consider twice about applying for a new Social Security number. Since credit reporting agencies can merge credit records with your old SSN with your new records, a new SSN does not guarantee a clean credit report.

IF YOUR IDENTITY IS STOLEN

Minimizing the disaster of identity theft depends primarily on your vigilant and constant efforts to guard your personal identification privacy, and thus be aware as quickly as possible that you've been the victim of an intrusion.

If you think you are or are about to become a victim of identity theft (for example, your wallet is lost or stolen, blank checks you have ordered do not get into the mail, or you are billed for charges you have not to make or on accounts you haven't open), you should act immediately to protect yourself. Here are the steps you should take, beginning when you first believe you are or may become the victim of identity theft:

1. Make contact with the creditors, insurers, services, and telecommunications providers. Examine the accounts and see whether they've been tampered with or if new accounts have been created under your name. Request to meet with someone in the protection or fraud department, and then submit a letter verifying your conversation. Any accounts that have been interfered with should be closed.

2. Report stolen checks. Report stolen checks to check authorization agencies. Different merchants report to different check authorization agencies, so reporting to as many as possible gives you the best chance of preventing your stolen checks from being used or cashed.

3. Request an initial fraud alert. You should request an initial fraud alert from one of the three nationwide credit reporting agencies as far as you think you have been or may soon be a victim of identity theft. You will have to give identity proof, which may include your Social Security number. The agency receiving the alert must notify the other two agencies, and all three must place an initial alert in your file for 90 days. You must not allow an extra card for an established account, an expansion in an existing account's credit cap, or fresh credit, according to the initial warning-able measures to confirm your identity, the alert may delay your ability to get credit. Each agency must also provide the alert each time it generates your credit score. You can get a free-cost credit report from each of the major agencies when you place an alert if you request it. If you discover that you don't need the alert, for example, because you found a missing credit card or check, you can ask to have the alert removed before 90 days have passed. Of course, you'll have to provide enough identifying information, so the agency knows it's you, and not the thief, asking that the alert be removed.

4. Close unaffected existing accounts. If you are the victim of identity theft, some privacy advocates recommend closing accounts that haven't been affected yet, on the theory that it's just a matter of time before the thief gets to those, too. It's best to take the cautious approach and close accounts

that the thief might otherwise be able to access. This could lead to problems, however: You might have trouble getting new credit or opening new accounts until the identity theft problem is resolved. Instead, you can notify creditors that you have been or may be a victim of identity theft, set up a new password, and ask that a fraud alert be placed on your accounts. Or, you could ask the creditor to cancel the old number and issue you a new credit card number on the affected account.

5. Review your credit report from each nationwide credit reporting agency. Check each report carefully, looking for accounts you didn't apply for or open, inquiries you didn't initiate, and defaults and delinquencies you didn't cause. Also, check your identifying information carefully.

6. Fill out the FTC's ID Theft Report at www.identitytheft.gov. The FTC recently overhauled its online identity theft victim assistance process. The new site is a one-stop resource that allows you to report identity theft and get a recovery plan.

7. Ask the agencies for credit reporting not to include information related to identity theft in your credit report. You can use the FTC's Sample Identity Theft Letter to a Credit Bureau, along with Section 605B of the Fair Credit Reporting Act as an enclosure. You must send each agency proof of your identity and theft of your identity report and your credit report with the disputed info. The agency normally must block reporting of the information within four days and inform the creditor that provided the information that it has been blocked. The creditor cannot then report the information or sell, transfer, or place the debt for collection. If you provide the same information to a check services company (a company that provides check authorizations), it cannot report any checks that you have shown resulted from identity theft to any nationwide credit reporting agency.

8. Request an extended fraud alert. You can ask any of the nationwide credit reporting agencies to place an extended alert in your file when you file your Identity Theft Report with that agency. That credit reporting agency must then provide this information to the other two nationwide credit reporting agencies. The extended warning is close to the original alert, but it lasts for seven years and obligates you to two free credit reports from each department for the following year. (in addition to the free report everyone is entitled to every twelve months). For five years, the agency must exclude you from lists it prepares for creditors or insurers who send out pre-screened offers (offers you didn't request). You may provide a telephone number or other contact information that creditors must use to confirm that any requests for credit in your name are actually made by you, not an identity thief.

9. Provide creditors proof of identity theft. Provide creditors a copy of your Identity Theft Report. Creditors may accept the Identity Theft Report as proof when you claim that you're not accountable for a fresh account or for transactions on an existing account. (Some creditors may require you to submit more information or use a different form.) Creditors can use this information to investigate your claim. Send the Identity Theft Report by certified mail, return receipt requested, and keep the originals of any supporting documents. You can use Form F-33, Identity Theft Dispute Letter for Existing Accounts, or Form-34, Identity Theft Dispute Letter for New Accounts.

Conclusion

Given the many issues with credit scoring, it's reasonable why certain individuals believe the method is fatally inaccurate. Any of my readers inform me they've ripped up their credit cards and are willing to live a credit-free existence because they're too mad with credit scores and lender actions in general.

Most of us, on the other hand, exist in a society where credit is practically a must. Some of us can afford to buy a house outright, while even more need loans to purchase automobiles. Credit may be used to start a new venture or pay for college. Credit cards are often common with Americans because of their ease. Although it is true that excessive credit usage can be tragic, credit used correctly will improve your existence.

If we want recognition, we must understand how credit scoring operates. Knowledge is strength, and the resources I'll offer you in this book will empower you to take control of your credit and finances.

www.ingramcontent.com/pod-product-compliance
Lightning Source LLC
Chambersburg PA
CBHW070809220526
45466CB00002B/608